THRACIAN PRINCESS

B T Johnson

First published 2007

This edition 2008

Copyright © Bistra Johnson 2007

The moral right of the author has been asserted

All characters and events in this publication, other than those clearly in the public domain, are fictitious and any resemblance to real persons living or dead is purely coincidental.

All rights reserved

No part of this publication may be reproduced, stored in a retrieval system, or transmitted in any form or by any means without the prior permission in writing of the publisher, nor be otherwise circulated in any form of binding or cover other than that in which it is published and without similar condition including this condition being imposed on the subsequent publisher.

ISBN: 978-0-9556875-0-1

To my husband
who helped me every step of the way

CONTENTS:

	INTRODUCTION	5
I	GOING EAST	8
II	LAND OF ANCIENT HISTORY	14
III	BACK IN TIME	21
IV	A ROYAL WEDDING	27
V	NEW LIFE	31
VI	THE GODS	36
VII	THRACIANS AND GREEKS	42
VIII	THRACIAN ART AND CRAFTS	46
IX	POLITICS	48
X	NEW EXPERIENCES	51
XI	THE WAR IN THE SOUTH	56
XII	ATHENIANS	62
XIII	TOUR OF THRACE	65
XIV	BOSPHORUS	70
XV	ALCIBIADES	74
XVI	HELLESPONT	78
XVII	THE TEMPLE OF DIONYSUS	83
XVIII	THE INITIATION OF SARATOCOS	86
XIX	MUSTERING THE TROOPS	89
XX	AN ENDING	91
XXI	BACK	95
XXII	ON THE TRAIL OF THE THRACIANS	100
XXIII	A NEW BEGINNING	115
XXIV	ENGLAND, ENGLAND	124
XXV	CHRISTMAS - PRESENT DAY THRACE	135
XXVI	VARIOUS VISITS AND EVENTS	146
	GLOSSARY	156
	BIBLIOGRAPHY	173

INTRODUCTION

Dreamy Veronica, Oxford University graduate, finds herself back in time and in true 'Alice in Wonderland' fashion, starts exploring her new surroundings. Following in her footsteps, we enter the uncharted territory of the ancient Thracians. The author hopes that this encounter with the distant past will fascinate her reader as much as it fascinated her while she was doing her research and writing the story.

This novel is entirely fictional, but is based on actual historical figures and events that took place in the Balkans during the 5th century BC at the time of the Peloponnesian war. The modern day characters and storylines are, of course, entirely the result of the author's imagination.

All the information concerning Thracian history, customs, mythology, religion, language etc. is taken from various sources, quoted at the end of the book.

The name "Thracians" is given to a group of tribes that inhabited the lands of present day Bulgaria and parts of modern Greece, Turkey, Romania and Macedonia between 4000 BC and the 6th century AD. Their civilisation is still shrouded in mystery, for they did not leave behind any written records.

Recently, numerous archaeological discoveries in Bulgaria have brought to light interesting facts about them. Prior to that, our knowledge of them mainly comes from Greek or Roman sources and these sources are not necessarily objective.

Far from being the bloodthirsty, belligerent barbarians they were portrayed as, the Thracians had developed a unique civilisation, a society based on a strict hierarchy with centralized political and priestly power. They were wealthy, powerful and influential. Mining, crafts, music, agriculture, viniculture were flourishing in their lands and so was trade; savage tribal societies could hardly boast of such achievements.

Expert metalworkers, the Thracians left behind exquisite collections of gold and silver artefacts, some of which so perfect that it's doubtful that they could be manufactured now, even using present day technologies. Excellent builders, their tumuli still stand to this day for us to marvel at. It can be safely assumed that the culture of the Thracians rivalled that of the ancient Greeks.

Thracian culture reached its zenith in 5th-4th century BC. The invasion of the peninsula by the Persians led by the legendary Xerxes (480-479 BC), in his war against the Greeks, perhaps contributed to the unification of the Thracian tribes under the leadership of the Odrysians. The Persians having been expulsed by the Greeks, the Thracian king Teres set himself the task of establishing a strong Thracian state.

Teres was not the first Thracian ruler, but was the first powerful king of the Odrysians. Under his and his successors' rule the Odrysian state became the dominant political and military alliance on the Balkans until the rise of the Macedonian kingdom. Seuthes I, the grandson of Teres, consolidated the mighty kingdom he'd inherited and brought it stability and affluence.

According to Thucydides, of all the kingdoms in Europe, between the Ionian Gulf and the Euxine, it was unsurpassed in revenue; both in terms of money and in general prosperity, and second only to the Scythians in military strength and army numbers. The archaeological evidence increasingly confirms this with more and more amazing finds seeing the light of day.

During Roman times, Thrace was a semi-autonomous province and was later incorporated into the Empire. Since then the name "Thrace" has only applied to the lands south of the Balkan range; the lands to the north becoming known as Moesia.

Dreamland is a different country. Anything is possible there. But this was more like a vision: a great hall illuminated only by the light of torches; a sumptuous feast fit for kings; a man with a golden mask sitting in the seat of honour - his elbow on the table, his head supported by his right hand; suddenly the mask is off his face and lo and behold: this is not actually a mask, although it looks like one, but a tankard full of wine that the man is drinking from. Who is this mysterious man? A big man with a reddish beard and short moustache, his knowing eyes sparkling with amusement as if at a joke that only he knew. He is beckoning to her...

But even as she was waking up, distracted by the real world and its demands, she lost hold of it and the dream dispersed like a morning mist with the advent of the day. She didn't recall it until much later. All that was on her mind at the time was her forthcoming trip.

GOING EAST

Veronica looked up at the building opposite – new, modern structure with a slender white turret reaching for the sky; somehow it stood out from the other multi-storey blocks of flats next to it. At the same time it conveyed a certain foreignness to her for some reason and she couldn't put her finger on why it was so. In a way it felt as if it were another universe, unlike anything she knew.

She wondered what had possessed her to rush like that to the other end of Europe. The avowed reason was that she wanted to see her parents right away and decided to spring a surprise on them, arriving unexpectedly to visit them at their new place, although strictly speaking it was not really theirs. They were just renting at the moment, while their house in a nearby village was being renovated. But Veronica felt that somehow they belonged here now.

She never thought that they would ever leave England. They seemed so well settled there and were not at all the adventurous type. However, after the building boom in Spain and France, the European Union opened up to Eastern European countries, starting the current trend for lots of Brits to take advantage of the situation and move eastwards where their pensions/investments would go much further.

Her parents also decided that their standard of living would be higher there and promptly moved to Bulgaria. A country 'discovered' only recently by Western Europeans; surprised by the beauty and variety of its countryside. Veronica's parents had been equally impressed on a previous holiday. The risk had paid off; so far everything was working out well for them.

Not so for Veronica though. She was going through what one could call a "bad patch". Just out of Oxford, where she had had such a great time, she was forced to face the grim reality.

Her bright ideas about her future gradually evaporating, it dawned on her that she had been seeing the world through rose tinted spectacles; her impressive diploma did not impress anybody (or at least nobody that mattered) and she could not find a suitable job in London (it had to be London, where else?).

People with experience were needed, but how to get this experience if nobody would give her a chance? Vicious circle! She did not have either the right connections or the right background and with the naivety of youth had never attempted to cultivate friendships that would help her later on.

Slowly realizing this it in turn made her so irritable that at length she quarrelled with her boyfriend and they split up; well, they both came up with the usual clichés; that each needed more space, that it was just temporary etc. but she knew it was the end.

No surprise she felt so disillusioned. In a time of uncertainties, when her little world was falling apart, she knew that she wanted her parents badly, she felt like the little girl again, in need of protection and security.

With these thoughts on her mind, Veronica picked up her suitcase and headed towards the building. As so often happens, her surprise did not quite work the way she had planned it. The "nobody home" scenario for some reason or another had never occurred to her. After ringing continuously on the intercom, she had to accept that her parents were out and she had not the slightest idea when they would be back.

It was a hot day and standing there in the full glare of the sun was not as pleasant as one might think. Her sun lotion out of reach on the bottom of her suitcase, visions of sunburn and skin cancer came to mind…

She reached for her mobile, wondering how much such a call

would set her back, when a smartly dressed man turned up. He produced a set of keys and proceeded to unlock the front door, saying something to her in the local lingo, which of course she did not understand. She replied in English and, luckily, he was able to speak to her in the same language.

It transpired that he lived in that very building and he let her in. It was nice and cool inside, marble tiles on the floor, their steps echoing in the silence.

They tried again ringing the doorbell of the flat where her parents stayed, but it was clear by now that they were not there. At that point the man, young and rather good looking she thought, invited her to his place so she could use his telephone and have some refreshment.

If such an invitation had been issued in England, Veronica would've been apprehensive and reluctant to accept. "Thou shalt not speak to strangers" was deeply ingrained in her mind. But as it was, she just felt grateful; she rather liked this Bulgarian, besides she was on holiday and also it had been a long day.

Veronica had flown from London to Sofia and then taken the coach to Stara Zagora, a city some 3 hours drive from the Bulgarian capital, to arrive finally in the late afternoon. She did not have chance to eat any lunch and, depressed or not, she still had what one might call a very healthy appetite.

Veronica smiled remembering her bewilderment at Sofia airport, where she hailed a taxi and shoved the note with her parents' address under the nose of the taxi driver.

"This Sofia taxi," he had muttered sullenly in very bad English, "no go Stara Zagora, go bus stop."

She hadn't realised that the distance was so great. But the taxi drove past some dreary concrete blocks of flats, reminders of the communist era, down a wide road up to the coach terminal where it left her.

Happily some basic English was spoken there; she boarded a

bus which took her to Stara Zagora and, eventually, after another taxi ride she arrived safely at her destination only to discover the absence of her parents. They could be anywhere! It was silly of her to presume that they would stay at home the whole day!

Presently her new acquaintance, who introduced himself as Peter, lifted her heavy suitcase with ease and escorted her to a neat, stylishly furnished apartment, situated on the top floor of the building – exactly in the very turret she had admired earlier.

It was what the Europeans would call a maisonette and offered a fine view towards the town. There were a few watercolours on the walls that attracted her attention, predominantly of churches and probably executed by the same hand, which, she guessed, must have been that of her host.

She was offered coffee, biscuits and cheese pastry, a local speciality, and she was also able to locate her parents on the phone. Of course they were astonished at her arrival and said they would be back shortly.

In the mean time she had a chat with Peter whom she found quite entertaining. He spoke English fairly well for a foreigner, which was a relief; she disliked foreigners who thought highly of their ability to master her mother tongue and who would blabber on in an incomprehensible fashion and then wonder at her blank expression.

Peter spoke slowly, that's true, but he kept the conversation going, and the time simply disappeared until her parents came and she took her leave.

It transpired that Peter was an architect with an interest in archaeology and very soon they were discussing Roman artefacts, which was a pet topic of hers and which unfortunately she was hardly able to discuss with anybody these days, and definitely not with James, her ex-boyfriend, who found it extremely boring.

Peter said that during the excavations for that very building they were in, the remains of a Roman villa had been discovered and even showed her some pictures to prove it, noticing the doubt that crossed her face.

She was quite impressed; it appeared that Stara Zagora had a long, long history; 8000 years he said, however she did find that hard to believe, but accepted it when it came clear that that was the age of the Neolithic dwellings nearby. The Romans had founded a town (known as Augusta Trajana) at some stage, near an earlier, Thracian, settlement called Beroe.

Veronica had visited a number of Roman sites in Britain but although she found this period of British history extremely interesting (indeed it formed a major part of her studies) on the whole she felt that it was sadly not appreciated by her contemporaries.

She joked that if they had lived in Roman times, when both of their countries were part of the Empire, they would have been able to freely move about between the two without visas or any such formalities. Peter found her remark highly amusing.

"And thousands of years later we are trying to accomplish the very same thing again in unifying Europe!" he replied.

So far, so good; girl met boy, both had similar interests and it could have turned out to be the usual holiday romance; but it was not meant to happen that way and Veronica could have no premonition of the adventure she would soon be involved in.

At that time she just thought that Peter was an interesting bloke, fun to be with and wondered if he fancied her. Since her split up with James, this was the first time she had been attracted to another man.

She looked at herself in the mirror, adjusting her dress and was pleased with what she saw – slim, blond with pale blue eyes and delicate features, the pastel colours of her dress in harmony with her fair skin, it would be a reasonable guess to say that she should appeal to Peter with his dark eyes and black hair. Opposites attract, don't they? She smiled at her reflection and the reflection smiled back.

"I think it's time to start dating again," she thought.

LAND OF ANCIENT HISTORY

The following day Veronica went with her parents to see their house. It was situated out of town at the very end of a pretty little village, called Zmeyovo, by a beautiful pine forest.

"It's so peaceful here," said her mother, "it's a place for old folks like ourselves. The young are gone to the big cities where the jobs are, some have even emigrated abroad. It's a bit sad."

"Won't they consider commuting?" asked Veronica.

"No, I don't think Bulgarians favour that kind of life style. Besides they don't want to be here."

"But it's lovely!"

"It is, but there is not a lot here to keep young people happy. It's not just the jobs; there are no amenities here to speak of; no entertainment; no restaurants, no bars, no cinema."

"You don't like commuting either," put in her father.

"No, I suppose not. It's not very green either."

"You see? Anyhow, for us all this is a good thing. We bought the house for a song, although it does need work and a lot of TLC of course. It's been neglected for a long time. But we are delighted with our purchase."

Lots of improvements had already been done and works were going to continue for another few months. But they hoped to move in before the end of the year.

Veronica thought that it would probably be nice to spend Christmas in such a place and tried to imagine how it would look in the snow; she might even try to take a break and come again for another visit. In the next few months she might even have a job!

Her father was concerned that there might be some delays; it appeared that during the work, while putting a new fence up, some metal trinkets had been discovered, in which the archaeology department of the local historical museum had shown a great interest.

However this seemed to be a single find, not part of a treasure trove, neither within a tomb, nor within the confines of a settlement. It was probably an offering to the gods or something of that sort. The experts had not yet dated it, but they were pretty sure that it was ancient, perhaps from Pre-Roman times.

"Gosh! How exciting! Already a find? An antique? No sooner do you start digging than you discover not any old junk, but a valuable object! Fertile land that!"

"I don't think I have ever found or won anything of any value in my life, so…" said her mother defensively.

"So, that's a start!"

Back in Stara Zagora, Veronica was taken sightseeing. They wandered around the centre and looked at the Roman remains. The ancient forum had been excavated and was apparently used today to stage performances in summer; one could walk down *decumano,* the Roman road running east-west, and imagine being back in time.

It must've been a major artery, judging by the deep grooves left by the wheels of chariots and carts. Roman artefacts always fascinated Veronica. She tried to imagine what it would have been like living in the ancient city. Walking down this road, heading for the theatre amidst a crowd of citizens wearing togas...

Her mother startled her from her reverie:

"Are you all right, love? Not too much sun I hope?"

Veronica reassured her, saying that she felt just fine and she liked it here very much indeed.

Moving on they then walked up a big but quiet boulevard, the road lanes divided by a pedestrian walkway lined on both sides with cypress trees; it was nice, shady and peaceful; pretty little water fountains here and there, elderly people sitting and talking, children playing, it felt almost like being in a time warp.

Veronica could well imagine that it hadn't changed much since the 50s though she wasn't even born then. But her mother turned her nose up at it saying:

"Not bad I suppose, but nothing more than an old fashioned residential area."

And Veronica smiled remembering that her mother did not like big towns and had always lived in a house in the country. However, she did appreciate what this town had to offer and was particularly taken by the beautiful park called Ayazmoto, where they were heading.

Veronica had to admit that it was attractive as parks go, apart from its name, Ayazmoto. Such a funny name that, it jarred somewhat; they could have come up with something that sounded better than that! Otherwise it was quite a place.

Apparently about a century earlier a local bishop came up with a grandiose project that resulted in these once bare hills being entirely covered by dense vegetation – trees and shrubs, crisscrossed by paths and alleys.

They had made a really good job of it. Some rare specimens were planted and many enthusiasts had since contributed with their labour or plants, until the park had taken on its present appearance.

Veronica and her parents wandered about the shady alleys, reached the tennis courts and stumbled across a bizarre structure, which turned out to be a hall of mirrors of all things! They had a good laugh while going round it. Her father's beer-gut exaggerated by the distortion looked absolutely hilarious; her mother's neck seemed elongated enough to match a giraffe's and Veronica's own dainty figure appeared as a really grotesque reflection! An illusory universe!

Afterwards they came to the zoo, which her mother though did not appreciate; she said it was a disgrace to keep all those animals in such confined quarters. But they all liked the young bear cub, which was such a happy little soul.

Veronica took lots of pictures of him to send to all her friends.

"It's all a question of the viewpoint, you know; we might see him behind the bars, but for him it's us who are behind bars!"

"Oh yes, you can say that. But you are missing the point, love. I don't think he is very comfortable in such surroundings. It's a barbaric way to keep wild animals in cages for our amusement!"

"But Mum, he enjoys himself, don't you see? He is born here, he doesn't know any other way of life! He is well looked after and seems to be in tiptop condition. In the wild he might not be so lucky."

"But he will be free!"

"Freedom is so relative. How much freedom have we got? Animals were captured and kept in cages since old times. The Romans for example, they would go to see them in the circus… By the way, to change the topic completely, Peter said there are some mineral baths just outside the town. Probably that was why the Romans came here in the first instance. You know how keen they were on mineral spas."

"Why? Do you want to go there?" her father was clearly amused.

"Of course! In the end you've chosen a rather nice place to live in, better take advantage of what it has to offer!"

"I hope you come to visit more often, so we could go and explore the area together," said her mother.

Veronica knew they would not venture far on their own.

Besides, once the house was finished, they would prefer to potter in the garden all day long.

She suddenly realised that her parents must have been pretty traumatised having to sell their house in England, when it became too difficult to maintain, so expensive. It was quite a big country house in Surrey and Veronica had lived there all her life before she went off to Oxford. And it was rather cluttered too. Her parents had to get rid of most of their possessions and it took lots of trips to charity shops, a car boot sale, and quite a few carloads to the rubbish dump.

She was saddened when she went to help them in the final stages to see the house bare and almost unrecognisable. She wished she had been spared that view.

Things were made worst for her when she split up with James and had to move out (they were living in his house). She felt that she had no home to go to.

Mandy, a childhood friend invited Veronica to stay in her place, till she sorted things out. But this was a temporary solution. She was relieved now that her parents at least were more settled and she did not have to worry about them for the time being. And she approved of their choice, sceptical as she was when she first heard about it.

All in all she was rather pleased with her little holiday; her worries all but forgotten, leaving her to reflect on the fact that some time 'away from it all' can do wonders for one's self-esteem and how on returning to England she was going to make a fresh start.

All right, it would be hard going to start with; she had left all her earthly belongings in the attic of her friend and she had first to find somewhere to rent (a mortgage was out of the question at the moment with property prices so high), but in a year or two, who knows, she might be able to afford a house of her own.

Veronica had already thought about possible areas, where she could go house hunting – Staines maybe or why not Windsor? She preferred Windsor, but it was probably not for her pocket. Still, she might be able to find something in that area.

Veronica could even picture the house of her dreams in her mind: not very big, but with a garden, one or two bedrooms, a walk-in-wardrobe (she always wanted one since she had been on holiday in America), nice patio where she could sit when the weather was nice and a garage, definitely a garage.

She suddenly felt homesick; or rather she had a very strong desire to be back in England, back to their dear old house, safe. The pain of realising the impossibility of it was overwhelming.

Veronica had been to the old family house only once since and she wished she had not. It was much altered. The hedge in front, pride and joy of her mother was gone to open more space for parking, not surprisingly for through the open garage door, she could see that it was only used for storage.

"Day-dreaming again?" said her father coming out onto the terrace where Veronica was sitting.

"Just admiring the sunset, Dad."

"Nice, isn't it? The beauty of this flat is in the two terraces, as I was pointing out to your Mum; from the other one you can admire the sun rise (not at the same time of course) for it faces east."

"Oh yes, I noticed that! I was up early today, remember? Couldn't sleep."

"Really? But it's so quiet here! It's double glazed, you know, you don't hear the traffic noise, besides the bedrooms face the back garden, not the main street."

"No, it wasn't the noise, Dad. I just had too much on my mind. And the traffic is not that bad. I saw you have a trolleybus passing in front. I am curious to go on it. Don't laugh; I have never been on such a contraption before! It looks quite funny with those poles sticking up, but from an ecological point of view, it's probably better than a bus. Maybe tomorrow I'll give it a try."

"Why not! But let's go in now. Dinner is out, let's not keep your Mum waiting."

BACK IN TIME

"To Nike, Fumigation from Manna.
O powerful Nike, by men desired,
With adverse breasts to dreadful fury fired,
Thee I invoke, whose might alone can quell
Contending rage and molestation fell.
'Tis thine in battle to confer the crown,
The victor's prize, the mark of sweet renown;
For thou rulest all things, Nike divine!
And glorious strife and joyful shouts are thine.
Come, mighty Goddess, and thy suppliant bless,
With sparkling eyes, elated with success;
May deeds illustrious thy protection claim,
And find, led by thee, immortal fame."
    The Orphic Hymn 32

The smoke was overwhelming; she gasped, she coughed, she tried in vain not to inhale it. Then she saw him. He stood not far from where she was, staring at her; a man of a most striking appearance. In fact he was probably the most handsome man, she had ever seen; big and strong and well built with startling blue eyes and fair hair; but strangely attired, "a knight in shining armour", straight out of an Arthurian legend, bearded and wearing his hair in a very peculiar style.

However she did not have the chance to reflect on it any longer for he rushed towards her and pulled her away from the fire. It happened so quickly! He then lifted her into his arms and with her head resting on that powerful muscular chest, took her away to safety where she could fill her lungs with fresh air.

She closed her eyes. It was all somewhat surreal; apart from him; he was real enough for she could hear his heart beating and feel his strength. But what had happened to her? It was as if she had suddenly found herself in some rather melodramatic novel of Barbara Cartland's; and it was getting even better.

Nearby a group of armoured knights on horseback were waiting, the man carrying her in his arms seemingly their leader (or rather their king judging from the golden insignia on his armour), nodded his head curtly and one of them jumped from his horse and held her while his master mounted his white stallion, a high spirited animal with proud posture and shimmering silver gilded harness.

Then she was lifted reverently up and found herself sitting in front of the king. There wasn't any saddle, just a soft saddle cloth through which she felt every movement of the horse which was a queer sensation.

The impatient horse did not have to wait long, an order was given by the king, something, which sounded to Veronica like *"poltyn"* and off they went, galloping away in clouds of dust.

"It's a dream," thought Veronica, "it has to be a dream or if not, I am an actress shooting some epic costume drama and this is the film set; it couldn't be anything else, it couldn't be!" she repeated to herself, "if it is, I must be suffering from amnesia or something, a nervous breakdown, perhaps? Because if not what the hell am I doing here?!"

But it all looked very authentic to her, the vivid colours, the country smell, the sound of the horses' hoofs, the perception of the agile body of the stallion beneath her and the mighty rider behind her; never heard of a nervous breakdown like this; neither was it likely that she was suffering from amnesia, for she remembered clearly everything that had happened to her recently.

She knew even her own name and said it aloud to herself: Veronica.

"Nike!" exclaimed her knight, pronouncing it noticeably like the last part of her name.

She said again: "Veronica." But he nodded his head enthusiastically and repeated "Nike, Nike" and Nike she was called from then on. Funny that Veronica should become Nike (Victoria), but was it really?

The name Veronica would've come from the Greek name *Pherenike*, which meant "bringing victory" from *"phero"*- "to bring" and *"nike"* -"victory". Of course these days they say it comes from the name of St. Veronica, the woman who wiped Jesus' face with her veil when he was taken along Via Dolorosa to be crucified; she noticed afterwards that on the veil had appeared a true image of the face of Christ.

So *"vera icon"* (Latin term *"vera"* meaning "true" and Greek term *"icon"* meaning "image") became "Veronica"; but would they combine Latin and Greek in one name? Not very likely, not in those times anyway.

These were the reflections passing through Nike's mind while they were galloping along. She was amused at her own nonchalance:

"It's a bit odd, isn't it? Riding a horse in the arms of a handsome stranger, as you do, and thinking about…the provenance of your own Christian name which actually happens to have pagan origins. Shouldn't you be at least a bit worried?"

Strange as it might seem, Nike wasn't afraid. She felt like a small porcelain doll in the firm grip of her warrior-king, so fragile, and yet so safe. She knew he would protect her.

But where was he taking her? Bewildered Nike looked around her – ahead lay a dusty track, on one side – a big field, on the other – extensive woodland. And they were travelling fast, almost as if trying to win a race.

She had little experience of horse riding, although she had ridden every now and then in Great Windsor Park, but never charging forward in this fashion, neither could she remember anybody else doing it.

She and her friends would go about slowly, chatting and laughing, careful not to tire their horses too much. And the ponies they used to ride in those days were rather spoilt creatures, which would not let anybody treat them this way.

Nike now wondered if someone was pursuing them but it seemed not to be the case. Perhaps they were just in a hurry or perhaps they found the rush of adrenalin exhilarating the way the driver of a MG convertible feels when they step on the pedal.

"What now? Perhaps we'll fight dragons, see a giant or meet an old witch? And reach an enchanted castle?"

Without meeting anything or anybody unusual, they arrived at the castle, fortified by thick high walls, heavily guarded by armed sentries. The gate was promptly opened for them and they entered a vast paved courtyard, in the middle of which stood what looked like a royal residence, a two storey stone building with an impressive entrance.

There were a few children playing around, but they disappeared quickly at the sight of the cavalcade. The knights dismounted their horses, the womenfolk appeared and she was left to their care; ushered into a room where she had a few minutes to recover from the journey and look around her.

Nike was dazzled. Her first exclamation was: "Wow!" followed by a second "wow!"

She had never, ever, seen such a collection of gold and silver in one place: vases, placed around the walls, jugs, bowls and lots of other objects, the function of which she could only guess at... How marvellous! A real Aladdin's cave! Yet it almost seemed like a *deja vu,* but where had she seen similar objects before?

She then recalled that recently she had been flicking through a leaflet, one of those tourist brochures, recommending a visit to the Historical Museum in Sofia and there were pictures of the magnificent Thracian Treasures that could be seen there.

Now Nike was looking at some of these, but not as a museum display. All these objects around her were new and polished and sparkling, not wearing the patina of many centuries, but recently manufactured, for use in everyday life.

"Gosh! What wouldn't an antiques expert give just to be in my place at this moment!"

Suddenly it dawned on her that she was actually in Thrace, the legendary land of Orpheus and Spartacus.

Nike knew of course where present day Stara Zagora was actually located, but somehow never gave it much thought. One does not think about legends in the day-to day grind. But now her classical education kicked-in and she viewed her circumstances in a different light.

The women entered the room again. Her clothes were taken away, stripped-naked she was washed and dressed in a magnificent garment; her soft, long blond hair was combed and arranged in a particular fashion, parted in the middle and at the rear gathered in plaits which fell to her shoulders; a gorgeous golden necklace was placed on her neck, bracelets on her hands.

And when Nike was presented with a golden-framed mirror to see her image, she could hardly recognise herself as the stunning creature that stared back at her.

"I've been contemplating having a complete makeover for some time. Now it seems I got more than I bargained for!"

She tried to speak to the women attending her, but to no avail. They did not seem to understand her and the language they spoke did not sound like anything she had ever heard.

Then Nike tried a couple of Latin words from her University course, but the women merely shook their heads; finally she came up with a Greek phrase that seemed to work.

Unfortunately their Greek language was difficult to understand; it did not appear at all like what she had studied.

Sometimes the spoken language differs significantly from the written one or maybe they had not taught her the proper pronunciation in the first place; anyway she had difficulties communicating.

Now she wished she had done better with her Greek studies but that was with hindsight, at the time she was not that bothered with it. At least one thing became clear though after this initial exchange – she had found herself in the Odrysian Royal Court, that is, in the Kingdom of one of the most powerful Thracian Tribes in antiquity.

It was hard to get used to the idea that she had gone back in time. All this H. G. Wells' stuff Nike had always found fascinating, but impossible to take seriously. Until now. Marooned in the distant past!

In fact, it was a very scary thought, but for some reason or another she did not feel at all scared. She felt exaltation like a young kid skiving off school for the first time and enjoying the taste of freedom; what's more, she had a sense of expectation, as if something wonderful was going to happen to her.

A ROYAL WEDDING

Nike was married to the handsome King Seuthes in a strange, pagan ceremony, which had a fairy tale quality. She did not have any doubts, any fears, she knew it was the right thing to do; Nike did not even consider that she had just met the man and did not speak his language. It felt like they were made for each other and as for the language, there might have been some Greek spoken between them but it did not matter, for they understood each other perfectly without the need for words.

A feast was held in their honour in the palace with music and dancing. The music was most enthralling and the dances – fascinating to watch. The guests, members of the royal family and other people of distinction were sat in a large circle. Most people with very few exceptions were wearing very colourful clothes - was it their "Sunday best" or their usual clothing?

Meat and bread loaves were piled on three-legged stools in front of the guests, tables were set conveniently around. Nike was surprised to see that the King set the example by personally breaking the loaves and meat and distributing them around, which was then followed by the others.

The Cupbearers brought in the beverage. The wine was generously poured out of golden *rhytons*; extraordinary vessels shaped like the head of a woman or animal with a second opening at the lower end, letting a thin stream of wine to flow into a *phiale*.

The wine itself or *zelas* as they called it was very fruity and very potent. And it flowed in abundance into the *phiales* of the assembled company. The eyes of Seuthes were sparkling, Nike felt his muscular arm encircling her waist and clasping her firmly.

It was not until much later she found out that Seuthes had two more wives, this being a polygamous society, but it would not have mattered for her in any case, because he had eyes only for her. And if there was nirvana in this life, she attained it with him on their wedding night.

One of Seuthes' wives was Stratonice, a serious and quiet woman, who was completely engrossed with her children, or at least such was the impression she created; on the other hand Meda, the other one, was mostly interested in running the household, which, to give her credit, she did very well.

If those two were not downright hostile to Nike, they were not overly friendly either. But such was the influence of Seuthes over his household that no display of discontent was ever shown, neither in his presence nor in his absence; which to be fair, was a rare occurrence, for wherever Seuthes went, Nike went with him.

If anything, Nike had the distinct impression that his other two women were rather pleased to see her go and be out of their way. To be sure they were probably jealous, but then again, they most certainly were used to it.

Talking to him at a later stage, when she was able to express herself better in Greek following a dispute between Stratonice and Meda, Nike enquired if it wasn't difficult to deal with so many women. He agreed that jealousy was always a problem, but if one expects more children to continue the family line, the more wives, the better chance his offspring to survive. Naturally a ruler like Seuthes would think for the future of his dynasty.

It should've been shocking for someone like her coming from the 21st century, yet Nike found it reasonable. Besides she was not ignorant of the fact that even in her times polygamy was far from extinct.

It was the intensity of her own feelings for him that surprised her; it seemed that theirs was indeed a match made in heaven. She wanted to be with him all the time.

As far as Nike was concerned Seuthes was an extraordinary man – a passionate lover, a caring husband, a courageous warrior and an astute ruler. She would not have expected all these qualities combined in a man living in such times. Or maybe living in such times had exactly shaped him into what he was. Whatever else though, Seuthes was absolute master of his own household and realm; an absolute monarch.

About forty years of age at the time, confident but never impetuous, Seuthes was a natural born leader if ever there was one. Everyone was eager to obey him, though he hardly ever raised his tone; there was this in him that compelled people to do so without much ado.

But Nike discovered pretty soon that his expression would soften and then brighten up when she was around; that he had an engaging smile, which others rarely saw, but which would appear on his face whenever his eyes met the eyes of Nike.

She realised that she had the rare opportunity to see a side of his character, which nobody else knew existed. This was the Seuthes she loved so much.

"In a way Seuthes has become my entire world now, my only friend, my confidant, my protector," Nike thought, "but who else can I trust? Who else cares about me in this world? I don't even have a family; my parents are not even born yet!"

Indeed her position as the favourite wife of a powerful ruler was a rather precarious one. It set her indisputably apart from the rest of the household and not withstanding all the privileges she had, kept her cut off from the others; not speaking the local language aggravated matters; she was looked on with distrust, as a foreigner usually is.

Of course she tried to be friendly with everybody in the royal household, but apart from the necessary civilities exchanged at each encounter, she never acquired any real friends.

Like most English, Nike was to a certain extent socially inept, that is she felt ill at ease in social situations. Taken away from her normal environment she was not unlike Dorothy when transported to the Land of Oz – completely out of her element; except that making friends was not so simple.

The Thracians might've been an easy going people but didn't quite know what to make of her and left her to her own devices. No surprise then that she poured all her love on Seuthes for he was a very willing recipient. Perhaps he really saw her as the goddess Nike reincarnated or perhaps it was just because she was so different from the women he'd known hitherto.

For a start most of the Thracian women were built on a larger scale, real Amazons, worthy of their men. Nike had a slight, dainty figure, very pale skin, a typical English rose; small feet, refined hands, the feet that rarely trod barefoot, the hands unused to manual labour.

Whatever the reason, Seuthes was bewitched by her. He expected her to accompany him everywhere, which suited her just fine; that was all she wanted for she only felt secure at his side.

Most fairy tales would end at this point: they got married and lived happily ever after; but this is not a fairy tale and the adventures of our young heroine have just begun. And not everything is what it seems; sometimes the end is a beginning and a beginning is the end…

NEW LIFE

Nike lost all sense of time. She was living in a wonderful dream. Surrounded by gold and silver she was waited upon and treated like royalty. In fact her status was that of a Thracian princess.

Somewhere out there people were working hard for their daily bread. But having married into the royal family Nike had dispensed with all this. For the first time in her life, her adult life that is, she was spared the worries of everyday living. And never once did she miss the technological wealth of the 21st century.

She rarely thought of her life before. Once upon a time she was the proud owner of a car, a computer and a mobile; a television set, a stereo and a digital camera. But she did not need any of these objects any more. There was a time when she could not imagine starting her day without checking her Emails, SMS, watching the Breakfast news on TV and then getting into her car.

Strange as it may sound, she was actually glad to be away from the hectic life of the 21st century. What a relief to be spared the little dilemmas of everyday life such as shopping, deciding on the meal in a restaurant, changing her Internet provider or the Christmas presents.

The Thracian world was a violent one. But Nike led a sheltered life. She was protected and looked after, she was loved and cherished. What was happening in the world generally she chose to ignore.

In her own century, TV had been providing her every day with a ration of murders, rape, wars and misery. There was always this sense of doom and gloom after watching the news. "Isn't there anything cheerful happening on this Earth?" she often thought.

Nike was now leading a life of luxury. There were lots of privileges in being a royal. Having servants to deal with all the mundane tasks was a whole new experience for her.

For the first time in her life, Nike had personal dressmakers, taking care of her wardrobe. They spent a lot of time taking measures, making the necessary adjustments until they got it perfect. She thought that it was most certainly the way a super model would feel, having all these people making such a fuss of her. Every single frock she got was unique, made especially for her and was more an object of art than a piece of clothing; some of the fabric was imported from far away countries, often decorated with exquisite embroidery. But then the wife of a king had to wear the very best.

Now Nike had the leisure to ruminate on a lot of topics. After rejecting various ideas she had stopped speculating how and why she'd found herself here. The one that Nike preferred the most was the escapist theory, but it had one serious flaw - she would not have chosen this particular world; she would most certainly have gone to ancient Rome! After long and fruitless speculations, she decided to turn her attention to something else. Shouldn't she just accept her present life as if it was a holiday?

Certainly it felt like one. And she enjoyed every moment of it. Out for a ride in an open carriage or rather a chariot as they were called, she was able to admire the absolutely unspoiled nature of those far away times. The actual ride was an overrated pleasure though; roads and carriages have come a long way since.

Having always lived in the densely populated South East of England, Nike found it at first strange and then refreshing to find herself in a peaceful countryside. Settlements here were few and far between and they somehow merged into the landscape in a way the modern city never could.

It was mostly dense forests that surrounded them on all sides and those forests were teeming with life: wolves, bears, wild boar, deer none were a rare sight. Seuthes said that there were lions too, but they had moved to the south; the climate was changing; it used to be milder in the past, but now the winters were becoming particularly severe and some animals could not survive.

Another climate change? Only in reverse. But then what about their CO_2 emissions? She would've thought her carbon footprint would not be that high but it was pointless to ask; neither chemistry nor climatology existed then, in whatever epoch it was, for Nike was not at all sure about the period she was living in. It was definitely prior to the Roman invasion of the Peninsula. The Latin language was not spoken here, neither were the Romans ever mentioned. Spartacus was not born yet!

Come to think about it, she thought that whatever Seuthes was saying the weather was warmer for early spring than what she was used to, though she was not even sure about the month neither could she make head nor tail of the calendar used; and she idly wondered what the weather in Britain might be at that moment. Or indeed who inhabited the British Isles? Have the Saxons already settled there? In fact no, it was far too early for them.

Probably it was still the Druids who had free reign there. Stonehenge would probably be in existence but not much more. She would speculate sometimes about all that, but it did not really matter to her one way or the other. Thrace was her home now.

It was a real treat to be able to explore the woods with Seuthes and they went out riding almost every day. Seuthes had reassured her that it was quite safe, though it had not always been so.

At one time the place was heaving with highway men preying on travellers and quick to relieve them of their belongings. But Seuthes had gotten rid of them.

"I remember having a lot of trouble with one of those thugs. A real fox he was, sneaking around and always slipping between our fingers when we tried to apprehend him."

Seuthes smiled at the memory. At this moment he looked almost boyish.

"We played this game of hide and seek for awhile and probably he would've still been at large; but his philandering with young women was his undoing. Women found him attractive for some inexplicable reason and he took full advantage of that.

Thus he had seduced a young shepherdess from this area. Unfortunately for him the girl decided to confide in her bosom friend. The bosom friend did not keep the secret, all became known to her mistress and consequently to myself. Our man came for a rendezvous, but instead of his sweetheart, he found a band of soldiers to arrest him. That was that."

"And now?"

"Now people roam this place unmolested. And you and I will do the same."

And so they did on numerous occasions and always something unexpected and exciting would happen. Sometimes they would see a stag, other times - a fox. And Seuthes was always telling her stories about the weird creatures living in the woods, about adventures and heroic deeds that allegedly took place round here.

There seemed to be an abundance of fire breathing dragons prowling somewhere out there, daring heroes to fight them in order to gain fair lady-wives and fabulous kingdoms to go with them as their reward! Seuthes was a good story teller. Pity that those stories were never written down.

One evening they were coming back at twilight when they heard a certain commotion going on somewhere very close. They went to investigate. There was a village in the valley below and finding a good vantage point they saw a big fire and a group of young men just below who seemed to be sending burning arrows towards the village.

Nike was rather alarmed. But to her amazement Seuthes started to laugh.

"Oh they are having a rather good time down there! Look at that house they are mostly targeting, I bet the village belle lives there!"

Seeing the blank expression on Nike's face, he hastened to explain:

"You don't know this custom, do you? It's quite popular in this country. On this day or rather evening, the young men start a fire and send their burning arrows in the courtyards of the girls they fancy.

Of course people have cleared those yards beforehand to prevent the fire spreading. The girls will gather the arrows tomorrow morning and will show them around with pride, especially the ones who had received quite a number of them. It's good fun that!"

"It's a bit like that with Valentines cards," thought Nike, "a notch tamer though; it might set your heart on fire but not your house! And young girls do boast about such things."

THE GODS

On another occasion they encountered a band of men wearing bizarre costumes heading for the nearby village. A motley crew they were and rather intimidating too. Some were wearing furry outfits and scary masks made of animal skins covering their heads and faces and reaching to their shoulders, bells ringing on their belts, while others were dressed like women and one was even carrying a basket with a baby doll in it. They were a noisy and boisterous lot but greeted Seuthes and Nike with respect and exchanged a few jokes before moving away.

From what Seuthes said Nike gathered that this procession had something to do with the days of Dionysus. Here in Thrace he was called Zagreus. The baby doll was representing Dionysus-Zagreus himself of course, prematurely born when his mother Semele having insisted on seeing her lover Zeus in his true form, full of thunder, lightning and all - she died of fear when her wish was granted.

Zeus kept the baby alive by carrying him in his thigh and when the time came the baby Dionysus was born. Dionysus was brought up by the Nymphs and later they became his loyal followers. So obviously that's whom those men in drag were representing. The others must be the Seilenoi and the satyrs who were his companions.

So the cult of Dionysus was widespread in Thrace; perhaps it even originated here. But Dionysus-Zagreus was just one of the many gods worshiped by the Thracians.

Nike often went with her husband to the settlement where they had first met, which was called Beroe (she recalled that Peter had mentioned it at the time as the Thracian name for Stara Zagora).

There were various temples and altars there and they would

make offerings to the gods. It seemed to her that those gods were particularly bloodthirsty, judging by the amount of sacrificial animals they expected.

Sacrificing the victims, usually young bullocks, was quite a ritual. In those moments Nike almost wished she was a vegetarian, so repugnant was the sight of the slaughter to her. Coming from different times and very much in the habit of buying her meat from a supermarket, all ready to use and nicely wrapped, had made her completely unprepared for such bloody spectacles.

After the sacrifice of the victim, the animal was disembowelled, the gods were given their due and then the rest was shared among the participants starting with the priest. Partaking in such a meal was a sort of communion with the gods.

She gathered that Seuthes was not simply the king, but also the supreme priest for his people and it was he who played the ultimate role during their religious rituals.

He expected Nike to be close by as a rule and often the smell of the blood and the incense made her dizzy. She suspected there was some narcotic in the oil for the lamps, for it affected the participants and brought them to a state of near ecstasy. She did not think much of that particular aspect of her new life, but there was nothing she could do about it.

Pouring libations at the altar was a different matter; Nike could tolerate that and almost get pleasure out of it. And she admired the regal way Seuthes would perform the rites, and also the exquisiteness of the silver *phiale* he used during the ceremony, exactly an object fit for a king-priest, she thought.

She remembered well her first appearance at Nikes' altar; for that was where she had been found originally in the midst of smoke that day and what, she wondered, did Seuthes think about it (he never referred to that first meeting). Did he take her for the goddess herself who had come in reply to his prayers? It was very likely.

Of course Nike was the goddess of victory and he always called her Nike. And the thought was not as presumptuous as it might seem. In the end a Thracian king was almost a god in his own right. She smiled at the thought.

Nike wasn't at all sure about some of the gods they were worshipping. There was quite a Pantheon of them – she was able to recognise some from Greek mythology (perhaps the Thracians had adopted some of the Greek gods and vice versa, the Greeks also had adopted some Thracian deities).

Apart from Dionysus-Zagreus, the god of wine, there was Ares, or Candaon as he was known here, the god of war, not so surprising a choice, coming from such fearless warriors; moreover he was allegedly also born in Thrace, and as for Artemis, she paraded here as Bendis, in her portrayal as the virginal huntress, appealing directly to the Thracian mentality.

Seuthes himself would swear on Hermes at times, but the way he perceived this god was not exactly in accordance with the Greek beliefs; he believed the Thracian kings were descended from Ermi (as they called him) and that Ermi bestowed them with the royal sceptre as a symbol of the supreme power they held. There was a connection with the sun cult too.

But most of the other gods were unknown to Nike and the picture was getting rather confusing.

There was Hero, the knight on horseback for example and he was worshipped as a god; she saw his images all over the place, but especially on armour or as bas-reliefs. Why is it that the figure of an armoured rider always appeals to people?

Take St. George for example, the patron saint of England; it seems he has always been very popular in these lands too (her parents had bought an icon with his image from a souvenir shop in Sofia and said they were spoilt for choice). Of course in the time of the Odrysians he was obviously not known as St.

George; later with the advent of Christianity he would be worshipped under that name.

And what about that particularly horrible looking deity, represented as a winged goddess? They had even a silver jug with her image in the palace; she held a dog by its paws in each hand and smiled sardonically.

Nike though that it might be the Great Mother Goddess, but she looked more like Hekate, the triple goddess of ancient Greece, whose role was a rather confusing one. Or perhaps she was Artemis, the goddess of hunting after all? Whoever she was, Nike did not like the looks of her; she had the feeling that those malevolent eyes were following her around and sneering at her.

There was also Cotys, a goddess worshipped by all Thracians; she seemed identical with the Phrygian Cybelé. Various facets of one and the same deity?

In the end she decided that this had to be a representation of a different aspect of the same goddess, Bendis, which was another name for the Great Mother Goddess, whose role was quite complex. It appeared that in this guise she was more of a moon goddess, judging by a night feast to honour her, which Nike attended some time later.

It took the form of a really exciting torch lit horse race. It happened to be a very dark night (by chance or by design), but it did not discourage the crowds coming to participate; in fact it made the whole spectacle even more impressive.

A cavalcade of young knights rode by, all of them carrying torches; the reflections of the red flames exaggerating the already ferocious expressions on their faces. The riders were passing the torches from hand to hand like expert jugglers while they were galloping along. Really spectacular!

The crowd was applauding them as any audience would! The feast ended with a late night procession to the sanctuary of the goddess. And there was Bendis herself, at least a worthy impersonator, wearing a pointed hat and boots made of fox skin and holding a spear; if she was around, no doubt she would've been chosen for the part of Xena, the warrior princess.

The cult of Bendis had spread across the borders. It certainly was popular in Athens; Nike remembered that Plato had mentioned celebrating the Bendideia in his "Republic".

A no less fascinating figure was Zalmoxis. Nike had some vague notions that he was a former slave of Pythagoras who on return to his native lands started a new cult.

It was said that in order to convince his people that there was an afterlife, he hid in a cavern and lived in it for three whole years; presumed dead, when he eventually reappeared again in their midst, they believed him to have been resurrected after dwelling in the Kingdom of Hades. Eventually he became the principal god for the Dacians.

In fact it appeared that his people, the Dacians, were none other than the Getae, a great Thracian tribe, which lived to the north of mount Hemus (the Balkan range).

Nike was surprised to find that he was worshipped elsewhere too. Zalmoxis was also seen as the god of the dead by the Odrysians. They had no fear of death for they believed they would go to the realm of Zalmoxis.

But what then of Orpheus? For most people in the present day he is largely known as the legendary musician who went all the way to Hades to fetch his wife Eurydice. But there was a lot more to Orpheus than that.

There seemed to be a real man behind the legend, a Thracian ruler who lived in earlier times. He was a founder of a cult related to the Dionysian one that was spread far and wide across the ancient world. But while the Dionysian cult was more orgiastic, Orphism was believed to be more spiritual.

So Nike was somewhat surprised not to see any particular evidence or practice of those renowned and mysterious Orphic rites; but it did not mean that they were not carried out however. Orphic gold tablets wouldn't be on display for everybody to see either.

Certainly Orpheus was well known here and was regarded as a god; which was to be expected because it was said that he had been precisely the king of the Odrysians. Were then the rites he allegedly initiated kept secret? In any case, those mysteries were the preserve of men, she would not be invited to take part in them anyway. In the end, according to the legend, that was the reason why those local women killed Orpheus in such a horrible fashion, feeling slighted and excluded from his teachings, they finally had their revenge on him.

Having pondered on the matter for some time, Nike decided that her husband was not likely to be an Orphic priest for he was not a vegetarian, while those who followed the teachings of Orpheus, the Orphics, allegedly became vegetarians, after a mysterious initiation during which raw flesh was consumed in honour of their one and only god, Zagreus-Dionysus.

According to the myth he was torn to pieces and eaten by the Titans, a fate not unlike that which befell Orpheus later. The Titans were subsequently killed by Zeus and mankind was born from their ashes; hence the dualistic nature of man (the divine aspect coming from Zagreus-Dionysus, the mortal one – from the Titans).

The Orphics were said to be forever striving to purify themselves and reach perfection; apart from leading extremely ascetic lives, they were supposed to avoid bloodshed at all cost. But their cult is so shrouded in mystery that no one knows for sure.

Now Seuthes, the dashing warlord who enjoyed life to the full did not somewhat fit into this picture. All that said, he still managed to surprise her in the end and made her wonder again about his beliefs; for all she knew he might have been a secret Orphic priest after all. Whatever the case, on this, as on other subjects, he kept his own council and Nike was not a one to pry into matters so private.

THRACIANS AND GREEKS

The religious ceremonies aside, Nike thought that all in all the Thracians were quite a sophisticated people. She had had very vague notions about them before and knew that they were regarded as belligerent barbarians by the Greeks, but now she was finding out that this was far from the reality.

True, Thracians would fight if they had to and they were respected for their valour and often recruited as mercenaries by their neighbours. There was also a lot of bickering going on between the various tribes, for they had very clannish attitudes; yet they would not pick a fight for the sake of it.

Seuthes and his predecessors had been trying to unify the country and had largely succeeded. The centralised leadership they had established was working for them rather well, but in complete contrast with the democratic system of the Athenians, their neighbours. Nevertheless the Thracians also had an advanced civilisation and a distinct culture. But they held radically different ideas to their Greek neighbours.

Nike was able to use her knowledge of Ancient Greece, gained from her University years, while talking to the Greek ambassadors at Seuthes court. Her discussions with one, Tropias were especially useful in helping her deduce the time period she found herself in, covering such topics as the ideas of Greek philosophers, many of whom she was familiar with.

New ways of thinking based on reason had been evolving in Greece at that time. Greeks had started to question their fundamental beliefs and a new science, philosophy, had emerged in an attempt to provide some answers.

However the life of the Thracians amidst whom Nike lived, was still ruled by strict social and religious values. Mythology was still the medium they used to provide supernatural explanations about "life, the universe and everything".

"I can't understand what some find in Prodicus, the rhetorician," Tropias was saying. "People flock to his school to hear him speaking, although he has such a disagreeable voice. He is only interested in the money. He opened his school for this purpose only. Can you believe that he charges his pupils 50 *drachmae* each?"

Nike wasn't very sure who exactly Prodicus was, but said she believed that he had some influence on Socrates. Tropias confirmed it:

"Oh yes, they say he was Socrates teacher. But satyr-like Socrates is a different kettle of fish altogether. He goes about barefooted, always wearing the same clothes and interrogates anybody he stumbles upon no matter where – at the market, at the gymnasia or at the workshops.

Once when I was in the market place, minding my own business, choosing fish at a fish stall, along comes our man and starts questioning my eating habits. He implies that I am an *opsophagos*! Me, *opsophagos*? Fancy that!

I like my fish, true, but always do things in moderation, always! *Meden agan* (Nothing in excess) as they say! The fish we get in Athens are marvellous, I wish I got the like of it here, but Thracians, they don't have our refinement, even when they eat fish they don't prepare it properly."

Nike remembered that the term *opsophagos* referred to somebody who was mad about fish. And that was something that was scorned at, no matter that fish were undoubtedly seen as a delicacy.

The people of Athens led almost ascetic lives, disapproved of any excess in food, drink or clothing. That also explains why they despised the sumptuous lifestyle of the Thracians, who were indulging in such things. Or perhaps they were just envious?

Meanwhile Tropias was still talking, indignant at Socrates' rebuke:

"Strange bird Socrates. Never opened a school of his own, doesn't even charge for his teaching. I don't know how he manages it, what does he live on? No wonder his wife Xanthipe complains constantly. He wouldn't write down his ideas either. And yet he is highly respected. But the man *I* had the highest respect for, was in fact Anaxagoras. He was the one who introduced philosophy to Athens."

"Anaxagoras?" wondered Nike. "Wasn't he the one who said something about the descent to Hades…?"

"…is the same from every place." Yes. He is the one. You've heard of him then. No wonder, he is well known everywhere. Was a close friend of Pericles, but just before the war got himself into trouble. Actually it was because of his friendship with Pericles that he suffered. The political opponents of Pericles attacked him and charged him with impiety, said he was denying the gods recognised by the State. By Zeus, it was a set-up. If anything they should have charged Socrates instead. Anyway, Anaxagoras was acquitted, but he was by then a broken man. He left Athens and died shortly afterwards at Lampascus."

The conversations with Tropias were a real eye-opener; they helped Nike to understand better the times she was living in. He would sneer at the ignorance of the Thracians and at their lack of interest in the philosophical ideas flourishing in Greece.

Seuthes meanwhile did not have much respect for his Athenian visitors either:

"All this sophistry is just a waste of time. The Athenians have little else to do if you ask me. Gazing at their own navels. Take Prodicus for example. Makes a big thing out of the correct use of words. Who cares? Is that so important? We can manage to understand each other one way or another. Some ridicule him of course; others take him seriously and are prepared to pay lots of money to hear his gobbledygook.

At least Socrates doesn't take himself so seriously. And I do agree that one should know oneself. But when in doubt going to the temple is the best course of action. I always get answers to all my questions there."

"But surely there is some value in what Prodicus says. Misunderstanding does occur, you know."

"True. It happens when you don't pay heed to what's being said. No, no, you can't convince me in the importance of such teachings, Nike. Not everybody is well versed, but if you can trust them, you'll find ways to converse without ever having to learn rhetoric."

Nike found such exchanges particularly enlightening. In her own century most people found abstract ideas difficult, if not impossible. It's the exact sciences that flourish.

Philosophy is rarely taught at schools in 21st century England. Isn't it needed any more? Surely in this day and age when the Church is losing ground, philosophy, ethics in particular, could provide a set of moral values for those in search of spiritual guidance…

"You might find such knowledge useless, but I think Prodicus is a clever man, although rather pessimistic I hear. He also teaches ethics, the importance of duty…"

"I can agree on the importance of performing one's duty, Nike. But to be taught ethics by an atheist? I don't know about that!"

From her encounter with the ancient world it seemed to Nike that while the Greeks were becoming more idealistic in certain respects but also more rational, the Thracians remained true to their traditions, yet no less pragmatic. That was fairly simplistic perhaps.

Anyway she felt Thracian society was much closer to her own, the society of the 21st century, perhaps because it was also rather materialistically orientated. Who was it that said evolution turns like a spiral?

THRACIAN ART AND CRAFTS

The lack of literature in Thracian society baffled Nike. Until she realised that it was their crafts that had taken over the function of expressing their ideas, beliefs and mythology.

She had noticed that all the artefacts in the royal house were lavishly decorated. The high quality of craftsmanship in the execution of these objects was surprising for such an early epoch. Each of them telling a story or having some symbolic meaning, which sometimes escaped her but nevertheless had significance for the local people.

The images depicted, predominantly portraits did not exactly narrate local myths the way it was done on Greek pottery; their message was much more subtle.

Nike could easily recognise the image of Dionysus for example on a golden *rhyton* (she had seen so many similar images on Greek vases) for he was much revered in these parts and some of the Dionysian rites were presented on other vessels. What more appropriate place for representing the god of wine than on a jug used for this very beverage?

Horse heads were a popular motif – hardly surprising. Thracians were always associated with horses. The horse was a sacred animal here. She knew people back where she came from who effectively worshipped their cars and in the end the horse is a much more amiable object of affection.

Hero - the warrior on horseback was another favoured motif, especially for representation on battle armour and horse tackle.

It was all a question of image really. A big butch fellow would like to display heroic figures on his armour or his horse harness, not unlike the Hell's Angels and the motifs they would display on their leather jackets and motorbikes for example.

As for tattoos, the Thracians were no strangers to their use nor to body piercing. Actually come to think about it, not that different from the Picts in Scotland in Roman times! Ideas and trends so much in vogue in the 21st century. Not much had changed it seemed over the centuries.

The lion on an appliqué obviously conveyed to the Thracians as much meaning as the Puma logo would do to Nike's contemporaries.

Once while in town, Nike had the chance to see a Thracian craftsman at work. It was fascinating to watch how deftly he handled the precious metal, shaping it into the desired form.

While there she got a set consisting of an exquisite gold necklace made out of a number of geometrically shaped beads; every second one joined to spherical pendants by tiny cylinders and a pair of crescent shaped earrings, the ensemble decorated with filigree work. She seriously doubted that 21st century technologies could produce anything so perfect!

Across the street at another small workshop Seuthes ordered a dagger to be wrought for him and he wanted it to be made to his specific requirements; a mould was produced for him to inspect and a long discussion followed until agreement was reached. The sheath was to be made of pure gold.

The Thracians obviously had lands rich in precious ores, judging from the amount of gold and silver they were able to extract from it.

Seuthes was minting his own coins as his father Sparadocus and his uncle Sitalkes had done before him. Seuthes' coins were made of silver and represented a galloping horseman wearing a *hiton* (not unlike a short toga) and a wind blown *chlamys* (a cloak) on his shoulders; in his raised right hand he was holding a spear.

Very appropriate, Nike thought, an image that matched exactly her view of her warrior-king. Some of the coins actually bore an image of Seuthes' profile, but she thought he looked much more handsome in real life.

POLITICS

Every now and then Seuthes would take Nike for a visit to the neighbouring nobility; that is governors of territories belonging to Seuthes or leaders of other Thracian tribes, lesser kings than Seuthes for he was accepted as the king of all Thrace.

There would be an exchange of gifts while re-enforcing existing treaties or conducting new ones under oath. These important treaties were carved in stone (in spite of the saying) and the stone slabs erected in suitable places so they could be seen and read (the Greek alphabet was always used but they were not necessarily written in the Greek language itself).

Lavish banquets were given in honour of the visitors and no expense was spared to make them feel welcome.

Seuthes had emphasized the importance of these visits. He had said that it was the way to build new military alliances or renew existing associations. Although he was related by marriage with most of these nobles (giving one's sister or daughter in marriage to an ally was customary in the ancient world), it was still important to keep them in check.

Exchanging gifts appeared to be a most important incentive to keep agreements and promises; especially in the Thracian world.

They had just celebrated the wedding of one of Seuthes' daughters and the leader of another Thracian clan. Everybody seemed very pleased, even the bride, who, Nike knew had been involved with another fellow from her fathers court. Seuthes had to give away a big dowry, but didn't mind at all because this served to seal the pact with the bridegroom, a most dependable ally in wartime.

Nike had asked innocently if people did not want peace above all; was it not better to establish more long-term peaceful relationships with the neighbours instead of continuous preparations for war. Seuthes had smiled and replied that he personally would much more prefer to consolidate his kingdom rather than involve himself in costly and often lengthy armed conflicts, the way his father and uncle had done, largely depleting the treasury in the process. He had done enough fighting in his life. However it was not that simple to make peace treaties that would last.

"Sparadocus, my father, Sitalkes, my uncle and the great Teres, their father before them did a lot for the unification of all Thrace. Trouble is, at times we tend to squabble between ourselves more often than even our Greek neighbours do. Even great rulers like Sparadocus and Sitalkes were not immune from such squabbles; they quarrelled once and my father went away to spend some time up north at the court of the mighty Scythians, but later on they settled their differences and he came back. In spite of everything, my predecessors have largely succeeded in creating a centralized state. They were all three of them great warriors and great sovereigns," Seuthes emphasized with justified pride and then added:

"What the Odrysian Kingdom is at this moment is mostly due to their efforts. I inherited a strong regime, holding supreme power over the other Thracian tribes and I intend to keep it that way".

Most of the other Thracian rulers did indeed recognise Seuthes as their leader. But there were still certain tribes especially in the mountains who did not acknowledge his authority. All the same they would not challenge him directly, as long as he left them alone.

Whatever the complicated relations with his various neighbours were, war remained by far the most profitable business as a rule; plunder seemed to pay better than farming or craftsmanship or trade; the smallest provocation was sufficient to cause an armed conflict; and the duty of the king was to protect his people.

His uncle had lost his life some years ago defending his realm in a war with the Triballi tribe; Seuthes, his successor had managed to establish peace with them afterwards. But for how long would it last? One could never tell. The Athenians were still at war with their neighbours, the Spartans, and he was concerned that they would involve him as well for he was their ally.

"So you see that is why it is so important to be always prepared for action with armed men and horses at my disposal."

Nike was reminded of a Latin proverb, succinctly stating: "*Si vis pacem, para bellum*" ("If you want peace, prepare for war"). The Romans obviously held the same opinion then.

She had to admit that "better safe than sorry" and approved Seuthes' caution. She understood that he would not go to war lightly unless it was forced upon him. Even in the 21st century, Nike thought, war was still a very profitable business and huge investments went into the so-called defence budget. But she was very ignorant of such matters, in which she was not that interested and preferred to explore this whole new world she had so miraculously found herself in.

NEW EXPERIENCES

During the summer they attended a festival held in the environs of Beroe. It was a warm evening and there was a big gathering near a mineral spring. Later on she would wonder if it was the same location as those mineral baths in the Stara Zagora of the future. But at that moment she was just taking in the whole scene. A huge fire was burning and a few people were dancing around it.

As the guests of honour they had the best places available and watched various dances, the allusion of which escaped her, cult dances of some description, maybe solar rituals. Such re-enactments of popular myths in order to speed-up certain processes of nature were not unusual for those times.

Though Nike did not think that the participants believed in the effect they were going to have on the weather, fertility or whatever it was, they just thoroughly enjoyed themselves the way people usually do at such events. It reminded her of a Carnival she had once attended in Nice, marking the beginning of Lent.

She was amazed by the variety of musical instruments of all shapes and sizes that were played during the show. Some of them she could identify as being similar to their contemporary equivalents (such as oboes, clarinets, guitars, timpani), others were absolutely unknown to her.

The festivities continued into the night and ended with a spectacular performance of a dance over the embers of a fire in a state of trance. She enjoyed the show very much.

Later, back home Nike tried to describe the festivities to the women who attended her. Limited as her vocabulary was, she somehow succeeded to convey to them the idea that the dancing girls were very pretty. One of the women said, so much the better for them, for pretty girls would be sold for a lot of money at a public auction to the men willing to pay for them. Noticing her astonishment, another of the women added that plain girls on the other hand had to buy themselves husbands.

Nike decided that either she had not properly understood what they were telling her, either they were just joking with her. Their faces looked pretty solemn though.

Reflecting on that conversation later, she decided that she should not judge these morals too harshly. What right did she have to do so when in her own time people would act in a similar fashion, only they were much too hypocritical to admit it.

How many "marriages of convenience" were performed every day that nobody ever questioned? Wasn't there even a case where a young woman was auctioning her own virginity on the Internet?

Besides morals were constantly changing with the times. Puritanical England of old, for example, was one thing, contemporary England - something entirely different.

Time was passing swiftly and imperceptibly; probably because Nike was enjoying herself. The royal court was a lively place, there was always something going on.

Once she was taken on a "shopping spree" as she called it, to a trading post, *emporium*, called Pistiros, situated on the banks of the river Hebrus amidst extensive vineyards. This was an exciting event.

They were escorted by a large group of knights and when they got there; their arrival caused quite a stir. The *emporitai* (traders) in this place were predominantly Greek, who obviously held the king in high esteem, something that she gathered from the way they fretted over showing him their merchandise.

To her delight, Nike got every single object she fancied as Seuthes was only too eager to oblige her.

How different was her life now! She could not help herself remembering the expression on James' face some time ago with a bank statement in his hand, complaining about being in the red, after buying her an expensive perfume for Christmas.

Perhaps this wasn't a fair comparison; James' meagre earnings were just not in the same league as the fabulous riches of Seuthes. In her disappointment Nike had become very harsh on poor James. With the realisation of the affection wasted on someone so totally unsuitable, the fond memories of their first months together were buried deep inside her, leaving only bitterness.

Nike was a sentimental person and wouldn't have married for money in any case; however having the means to indulge her and also showing the willingness to please her, had increased the regard she held for her husband.

She might be renouncing the materialistic pursuits of her contemporaries, but still as a child of her time, she highly appreciated what she was given. She also enjoyed the "royal treatment".

Seuthes explained to her later that the merchants were under his protection; they had a contract with him, concluded under oath. However, as the king owned the land on which the emporia were built, he received customs duties from the import and export of merchandise both from the Greek and the Thracian traders involved.

Nike saw even the stone slab in the centre of Pistiros, on which the full terms of this agreement were inscribed, starting with an appeal to the god Dionysus himself to witness the oath taken and then going into the minutiae not only of the dealings between the *emporitai*, the local authorities and the local populace, but also amongst the *emporitai* themselves. In short they were granted limited autonomy to freely pursue their trade, as long as they followed the law.

Being the wife of a powerful ruler Nike attracted a group of followers willing to be her protégés. At first she was very flattered, but then she realised she had to tread extremely carefully, for they were all after some benefit of one sort or another and expected her to speak on their behalf to her husband.

Take the Greeks for example; in those times they called themselves Hellenes, although first and foremost they regarded themselves as citizens of the respective *polis* (city-state) they came from. When Nike was presented to the ambassadors from Athens at Seuthes court, she was very pleased.

They were a very charming bunch and in the early days she'd quite enjoyed talking to them. But having to express herself in their language put her at a disadvantage because she was not very fluent in it and so they adopted a rather patronising attitude towards her.

Besides, the Athenians prided themselves in their masterly use of rhetoric and would try to impress her with lengthy and very elaborate speeches of which Nike would understand very little. She thought that they just revelled in the sound of their own voices and would go on and on extremely pleased with themselves.

Later on she found out that they played an even more sinister game as far as diplomatic dealings were concerned. Their main aim was in fact to spread dissent among the then unified Thracian tribes. Divide and rule as they say!

Seuthes told her once that he had given one of his sisters in marriage to the leader of the Paeonians. She was reported to have died in childbirth.

"It happens," said Seuthes, "in the end that was the wish of the Gods. I lost two wives myself in childbirth and another one after a miscarriage. But along comes this Athenian, Theorus, who had stayed with the Paeonians for a while and he says there was foul play involved. He says this not to my face either, but to others who he knows would tell me. I ask myself why – but it's obvious, isn't it It's known that tribes had fought for lesser cause than that. I didn't believe him but I might have."

THE WAR IN THE SOUTH

Some reports from Athens of a different nature had also come to Nike's attention. She was already aware that there was an armed conflict between Athens and Lacedaemon (that's what Sparta was called in those times); and it had been going on for years. The Odrysians were siding with the Athenians thus the Athenian presence at court.

Nike asked Seuthes to tell her more about this conflict. He explained to her that his uncle Sitalkes had been allied with the Athenians since the beginning of the war and they had all marched to the Chalcidian Peninsula (the three fingered hand like strip of land near the present day Thessalonica) to fight the Macedonians some time ago. Further more his cousin Satok, Sitalkes' son, and later Seuthes himself, were made honorary Athenian citizens as a sign of friendship.

"It was all for political reasons, of course. And they make use of this to pressurize us when needed. At the time when we received an envoy from Lacedaemon trying to persuade my uncle to renounce his alliance with Athens and help them instead, the Athenian ambassadors at our court convinced Satok, my cousin, to hand them the Lacedaemons, before they could leave for Persia, where they intended to ask for the help of the Persian King.

Satok was put in an impossible situation. It's a question of honour that we keep our agreements. So his men seized the Lacedaemons when they were still on our territory, heading to the coast in an attempt to cross the Hellespont, and promptly handed them to the Athenian ambassadors who took them to Athens. They were put to death there right away without being given as much as a trial. There is Athenian democracy for you. And they dare accuse us of being the barbarians!"

Nike knew of the Peloponnesian war, if indeed that was the

war in question, but she could not remember exactly when it had happened; a couple of centuries BC was all she could come up with. But it had given her a pointer and it was precisely what she needed. From what she had heard it was clear that the war was still continuing and had been going on for the last 21 years. She asked Seuthes to tell her more about the Thracian involvement in the war. This was the story he told her:

"It was at the very outset of the war when I was sent up north on a diplomatic mission to the Scythians, my father, Sparadocus having spent some time at their court in the past. Meanwhile events were unfolding fast. The first person I bumped into on my return, was Nymphodoros, a brother in law of my uncle Sitalkes and a close friend of his. I was surprised to find him there.

"Ah, big things are afoot, Seuthes," he said, "otherwise I wouldn't leave lightly my native Abdera. But I had to go to Athens. And guess what? They've sent me here with a mission, which, I am pleased to say, I duly accomplished. Sitalkes is to become Athenian ally and to give them a hand in the war with the Lacedaemons."

Apparently the Athenians had gone to all this trouble to get Nymphodoros to Athens, knowing well that he had influence with Sitalkes, and coerce him into favouring their cause. They must've been really desperate to have Sitalkes on their side, for Nymphodoros was certainly not a friend of theirs to start with.

However he became their intermediary who concluded the alliance with Sitalkes, also procuring Athenian citizenship for Sitalkes' son Satok. Nymphodoros had also taken it upon himself to persuade Sitalkes into sending an army to join the Athenian forces.

Sitalkes for his part succeeded in obtaining a promise from Perdiccas, son of Alexander and king of Macedon, to join the alliance too, if Sitalkes would reconcile him with the Athenians and renounce his efforts to restore Perdiccas' brother Philip or his son Amyntas to the Macedonian throne (Amyntas was at this point living in exile at our court, but his father in meantime had passed away).

However Perdiccas despite making such a promise was somewhat reluctant to keep it (he had never been very reliable, changing his mind with the wind). Sitalkes wondered if he could still make use of Amyntas as a bargaining chip.

Such was the situation when in the second year of the war we organised a campaign in response to the Athenian appeal for help. It took us some time, though it was not difficult to rally our people.

Sitalkes was such a great hero, worshipped by us all, so it was not a surprise that so many warriors should come along from all over Thrace! We mustered some 150 000 men in total of which 100 000 *peltasts* (infantry) and 50 000 cavalry.

With Sitalkes at the head of this substantial army, myself as his second in command and accompanied by Hagnon, an Athenian general, some Athenian ambassadors and Amyntas, Perdiccas' nephew, we set off on our march. Candaon, who protects the brave, was watching over us.

More and more volunteers were joining our force as we were heading south. We had to fell trees and open a wider road in order to ease the passage of our armed forces. Quite a task! This slowed us down even more but it had to be done.

Congregating in Doberus, we prepared to invade Perdiccas' realm. Now, the Macedonians did not dare to face such a formidable force as ours and retreated very quickly into their fortresses, taking grain, and whatever other provisions they could put their hands on, with them.

Their fortresses were not so numerous at that time (quite a few new ones have been constructed since), but never the less offered them protection. From there they launched only a few pathetic half-hearted skirmishes that did not accomplish much, apart from proving our superiority. It was obvious that they did not stand a chance!

We took Idomene by assault, while Gortynia, Atalanta and a few other fortresses succumbed mainly for Amyntas' sake. Amyntas was a dashing young warrior, very popular in his homeland and seen as being unfairly treated by his uncle Perdiccas; luckily we had him with us; his successful dealings saved us some trouble.

Anyway the Athenians, our allies, were to bring reinforcements by sea, for this had been agreed on. General Hagnon had been with us all along for the very purpose of leading them. Nevertheless it did not happen; although they did send us envoys and presents."

Nike was surprised:

"But why? They expected you, didn't they?"

"They did expect us, but not so late in the season; allegedly they waited and waited and they thought we were not coming after all. At least that was the explanation given to us. But was it really true? One can never be certain with them!

Anyway! Even without their assistance, nobody dared to oppose our advancement when we invaded the Chalcidian peninsula and forced the frightened populace to withdraw inside their walls.

I guess we were far too pleased with ourselves after our easy victory. We were still a bit put out that the Athenians did not turn up, but so much the better, for we were to claim the full credit for the victory; what else does a soldier live for but for glory? All of Greece was petrified at that stage and was mulling over who we were going to strike next.

If you ask me, the Athenians had made a grave error of judgement not sending the promised reinforcements; no matter was it because they did not expect us to keep our promise or for some other reason we knew nothing about.

If Pericles was still alive, things would have been different, I am sure. He was an astute leader; he knew where his interests lay. But as fate would have it and the gods of course, he had recently died, taken by the plague, ravaging Attica at the time. Very sad!" Seuthes sighed.

"And time was running out for us. As I said quite intoxicated by our triumph as we were, with the winter setting in earlier than usual, we suddenly realised that we were in deep trouble.

It happened to be an unusually cold winter and as one could imagine, we were short of provisions, even though we had ravaged the countryside and got what we could from the local inhabitants.

The purple-winged god Boreas was sweeping down from the north across the plain, chilling the air with his frosty breath; no matter how well dressed (most of us wearing fox fur caps, long coats under our capes and boots made of deerskin), we all suffered from the cold.

Even the water and the wine froze in their vessels when brought to the table. Worst of all we did not have enough food. It is not so easy to provide for about 150 000 men in the throws of a most bitter winter amidst a hostile populace. One third of our army was cavalry so we needed hay for the horses too. Everything was covered by the snow.

We reflected on the best course of action. While in this quandary, I received a secret envoy from Perdiccas, offering me his sister in marriage and a rich dowry if I persuaded Sitalkes to withdraw! This was a chance not to be missed.

I openly admitted to Sitalkes that Perdiccas was trying to buy me off. But why not take advantage of the offer, I reasoned? So we sat down and discussed the situation at length. Sitalkes was doubtful at first, but then I got my point across to him.

It was quite obvious what Perdiccas feared. He did not feel very secure behind the walls of Pella, his capital. We were getting desperate and might go for him in earnest to finish him off. But this would not solve our problem, we still had to feed 150 000 people or so, not to mention the horses.

So finally we arrived at the conclusion that we were not reaching our objectives in any case, our people were suffering the hardships of winter, the Athenians were not coming and furthermore our enemies were mustering armies to fight us.

We did not have anything to lose, so eventually we came to terms with Perdiccas to withdraw back to Thrace. Accordingly I was given Stratonice, Perdiccas' sister in marriage as promised and Perdiccas himself joined the Athenians as their ally; at least he did for that moment."

Nike listened to Seuthes' narrative with great interest. Stratonice was a stern woman who had borne many of Seuthes children and who kept herself to herself, so Nike hardly ever spoke to her and until then was unaware of her Macedonian origins.

She found all this really intriguing. So it appeared that Seuthes' children were closely related to the Macedonian royal family. Nike wondered about the time line. This must be a period prior to the birth of Alexander the Great. The father of Perdiccas was called Alexander and his brother – Philip, both evidently prevalent names in the Macedonian Royal Dynasty, belonging no doubt to the ancestors of the great conqueror.

The Peloponnesian war had most certainly taken place before the time of Alexander the Great. His hour of glory was yet to come!

ATHENIANS

Talking to the Athenians Nike had also picked up some gossip about certain Athenian politicians that she previously knew nothing about; especially about one Callias, a real black sheep, if there ever was one, who apparently came from an old and wealthy family, was the richest man in Greece but had lost almost everything, was left with barely two Athenian talents (currency) as a result of his excesses - sumptuous banquets and women. When Nike told Seuthes what she'd just learned, he exclaimed:

"You shouldn't believe everything you hear from these people, Nike. They are a bunch of hypocrites. They would've loved to participate in those banquets. In fact they most certainly did.

Callias is a most generous person. But if he lost his wealth it is mainly as a result of the war, rather than his so called excess. I know Callias well and he is probably the only Athenian who I would call a friend."

"They say he's a lady's man too..."

"Oh, well...they would say that wouldn't they? But they are all like that! They are having a go at us for holding on to a polygamous society, but in practice they have affairs all the time with different women, while their own wives are kept at home and hardly ever leave the house save for going to the temple.

The Athenian men in the mean time are chasing after *hetaerae* (courtesans) or the so called "flute" girls or just ordinary prostitutes...even somebody else's wife. But there is always a price to pay. Those women don't come cheap, you know.

Here in Thrace we might have more than one wife each, but our women are well looked after and do not have to sell themselves for money...

The trouble with Callias is that he is far too romantic for his own good. I told him this once. As I said, I regard him as a friend. I've taken part in some of his "extravagant" banquets and found them very enjoyable; met some interesting people there, such as Socrates and his bunch.

What's the point of being rich if you cannot have your mates round for a good meal? But Callias is too trusting and has lots of parasites around him who call themselves his friends.

One of them frequently invited Callias to his place and Callias found his wife irresistible. If you ask me, the wife seduced him on purpose and arranged with her husband to catch them *"in flagrante"*.

Now there are strict laws in Athens and a man caught in the act might be killed by the husband/father of the woman; however some arrangement could be agreed on; involving lots of money of course. That's what happened there."

Chit-chat with the Athenians was all well and good, but they also tried to bribe Nike with presents, though she had enough sense not to accept them. Offering presents in exchange for anticipated assistance was customary at court, but presents for a married woman were to be presented to her husband; otherwise it would appear she was acting behind his back and that would displease him.

Nike gauged these little subtleties more by intuition than by learning, though perhaps some credit should be given to her classical education; in the back of her mind undoubtedly lurked a warning to fear the Greeks even when bearing gifts (*"Timeo Danaos et dona ferentes"*). Whatever the reason in the end she started to distrust anybody who was too friendly with her.

Her sympathy was awoken however when a young Greek trader, who had supplied salt to the royal household, was left waiting for payment and was rather out of pocket. One of Seuthes deputies was stringing him along for no good reason.

Salt, it appeared, was a rare commodity and therefore very expensive.

"It's not as if the king Seuthes is in need of money and cannot afford to pay," complained the Greek. "They say he is one of the richest men around; his takings are rumoured to reach up to 400 *talents* annually in gold and silver just from *phoros* (tribute) and he gets as much again in various *dora* (gifts), not to mention all the fine cloth, plain or embroidered that he obtains for himself and his family.

You are wearing a beautiful frock, my Lady, but the stuff it was made of comes from afar. I bet you have plenty more and to spare. Speak to the King on my behalf, he won't refuse you, I'm sure. And may the golden-throned Hera, the protectrice of all women, watch over you."

Was 400 *talents* then such a considerable sum? It must have been, otherwise would it be quoted as if it were a fortune? But for Nike it was just a figure. However she made sure the Greek trader got his due (he was paid partly in cash, partly in goods) before he left.

He was a nice person, that Greek trader; with dark expressive eyes, dark hair and the typical Greek nose, that is to say big and slightly hooked. Nike found him very easy going but by that time she had become rather suspicious towards anybody who was too friendly, so she wasn't sorry to see him go.

Besides, she had noticed that Seuthes was not very pleased when she received attentions from other men; not that he ever said anything, but a sensitive girl like Nike was able to read his moods.

In the end Seuthes was not perfect, he was a great man no doubt, but rather austere and possessive and he never displayed any sense of humour, which Nike thought was a pity; although the truth is that one rarely attempts to joke in a language not their own unless they have complete mastery of that language and the confidence that they can carry it through.

TOUR OF THRACE

Nike learnt that Seuthes had other residences, as well as the one they were presently occupying, when he casually announced that he was going to take her on a tour of them. She was very excited for she loved travelling. Nike was aware of course that Seuthes wasn't taking her on a touring holiday but had other ideas in mind; never the less she would take full advantage of the occasion to see more of his lands.

It was going to be a lengthy journey, although Nike was unsure as to the extent of the Odrysian lands. It was not any clearer to her even after Seuthes' explanations.

It seemed that from Abdera in the south (on the Aegean) it reached up to the Danube in the north; an able man needed 11 days if travelling by the shortest road; it also extended from Byzantium in the east, to the Strymon River in the west; for such a journey one had to count on 13 days for an able man.

As Seuthes had obviously no idea of miles or kilometres, Nike left the matter to rest there and relied solely upon her own senses to decide on the distances.

So the journey took them all around his kingdom through a landscape that constantly varied. They were accompanied by a big cavalcade that grew even more as various new additions of horsemen joined them on the way. Envoys were coming and going and there was a burst of activity wherever they went, up around the mountains and through the valleys or along the seacoast.

At the entrance of some of the towns they passed, Seuthes was frequently offered a *phiale* filled with wine, as recognition of his leadership. These *phiales* appeared to be made especially for the occasion because both his name and the name of the town were inscribed on them. And he got to keep them as a memento.

These visits were always joyous events and Nike was extremely proud of her husband and his popularity. She was also amused to think of herself in such cases as being the escort of a great public figure; like doing the rounds in a pre-electoral campaign.

Nike was presented to the local nobility as they enjoyed sumptuous feasts at each stage of their journey. Seuthes referred to the people he invited as "table companions" and she understood it to be a special privilege to be one of the participants.

Seuthes always played the host no matter in whose house they were staying. The host was as always the one distributing the food; and according to Thracian custom he and his guests would pledge themselves in bowls of wine; toasts were held, the cups were emptied and the last drops were sprinkled fraternally.

But no matter how much Seuthes drank, he never seemed the least bit intoxicated; just a little more laid back and relaxed.

There was music of course. Seuthes might even take part in the dancing at times; he would do that with his usual sprightly step, remarkable for such a large man.

Those dancing were quite a sight; at one occasion they were performing a military dance to the sounds of a flute, holding their weapons and attacking each other as if in a real fight; some fell and their vanquishers took their weapons and withdrew, singing songs in honour of Seuthes. It seemed that one of the dancers was actually killed or at least seriously injured. The others lifted his body in a ritualistic way but hey presto: he suddenly sprang back to life and started to chase them in his turn! It was so entertaining!

But all this social activity was not just for pleasure. Important political, military and administrative matters were discussed at these feasts and she would notice every now and then a haggard expression appear on her husband's face.

Knowing neither the local language nor the current politics, Nike was unable to offer him advice or consolation but neither did he seem to expect them from her. So at such moments she tried to show at least understanding and solicitude.

They reached the sea, nowadays the Black Sea but known in ancient times as Pontus Euxinus (the welcoming sea). Its sandy beaches were then, as always, very alluring, but sunbathing was not in fashion in those times. Only fishing boats could be seen around, and occasionally a merchants' ship, the shores were otherwise quiet and serene.

They visited a Greek coastal colony called Apollonia Pontica. The main part of the town was situated on a small island not far from the shore.

There stood the temple of Apollo the patron of the town. Once in the temple your eyes were instantly drawn to a colossal statue of the god himself, made of bronze. It was probably more then 10-15 m high (20 cubits high they said, whatever that was)! Especially breathtaking if you did not expect to stumble upon such an impressive work of art around there.

Nike was told that the statue was made by the famous Calamis and it was valued at 500 talents which was a hell of a lot of money, but everyone deemed it well worth it. It did seem quite costly she had to admit, bearing in mind that Seuthes was getting annual tribute amounting to 400 talents and he was thought of as fabulously rich!

In the temple of Apollo, Nike also observed a marble slab placed in such a way for all to see, with an inscription in Greek, as a reminder (or proof) of the agreement between the Apollonians and Seuthes.

Nike did not understand it all, but from what she could gather, it started by singing the praises of Seuthes, a resolution that he should be crowned with a golden wreath during the Dionysus festival, given Apollonian citizenship and some other privileges for both him and any issue of his; and in turn his agreement to allow any Apollonian to enter his territory by ship for which he, Seuthes would be paid a certain amount of *staters* etc. etc.; quite a comprehensive contract between the two sides.

Seuthes apparently received taxes from the Greek colonies for keeping the peace along the borders (the so called *phoros,* equivalent of the Council tax maybe?) and in exchange the Greek colonists would ask him every now and then for support against their enemies.

He mentioned casually that he was getting quite a healthy sum from the colonies and a quantity of manufactured articles and ornaments besides.

Heading south, they reached Salmydessus, a desolate place with a stony beach exposed to the elements, as Seuthes appropriately remarked the home of Boreas, the god of the North wind. Apparently also a place notorious for ship-wrecking due to the shallow waters.

And where a very "Jamaica Inn" type of scenario would occur, the locals taking full advantage of the situation to gather the flotsam and jetsam coming to them, to the point that they had even divided the coast line between them, so each could benefit equally from what the sea had to offer.

From here the cavalcade proceeded towards Byzie, one of the main settlements in the Odrysian kingdom, apparently the main residence of the great king Teres, the grandfather of Seuthes. It was situated on a hill and offered a splendid panorama of the surrounding countryside, a vast plain with numerous mounds of earth scattered about it.

Seuthes explained that these were tumuli belonging to his people. Nike remarked on the circular plan of the tombs and wondered if that was a more sound structure than the rectangular one. Seuthes looked surprised:

"My builders certainly vouch for that, but surely you are aware of the symbolic meaning of the circle? The circle expresses the beginning and the end, life and death; it also symbolises the Great Mother Goddess..."

Then they resumed their journey and Nike noticed that Seuthes became more and more cautious as they advanced southwards. They spent the night in a well guarded fortification and the horses stood around in a circle; the poor things were fed during the day instead of being left to graze.

When questioned, Seuthes explained to her that these lands were not safe. In old times his grandfather, the legendary king Teres, had arrived with a large army and had suffered great losses at the hands of the local tribe, not to mention that he'd been robbed of his baggage train.

These local people, the Thynians, were notorious as ferocious fighters who tended to attack their enemy at night.

During Sitalkes' lifetime (that's Seuthes uncle, the previous king) they were forced to accept his sovereignty, but in recent times Seuthes had again had troubles with them, or rather with some of them, who remained stubbornly independent and were causing problems for everybody - Thracians and Hellenes alike.

They wouldn't risk an open offensive with him, because they feared him, but never the less, he had to tread carefully while in their neighbourhood.

Seuthes posted his troops around as sentries, but in such a way, that their fires were in front of them instead of behind them; so anybody coming towards them would be confused as to their whereabouts, but would also expose themselves to the glow of the fires.

It was not unlike stepping into the limelight when on stage and not being able to see the audience in the darkness beyond. A clever trick that, come to think of it! It was wise to be cautious and they pursued their route unmolested.

BOSPHORUS

At length the cavalcade reached the Thracian Bosphorus; the straits between Europe and Asia. Various myths come to mind in connection with it. The name Bosphorus means "ox ford," named so they say, after legendary Io, who in the guise of a white heifer had crossed the straits to escape Hera's wrath.

Hera, the wife of Zeus had discovered that he had had an affair with this pretty maiden and although he tried to save Io, altering her form, Hera recognised her and sent a gadfly to harass her and chase her away.

The Ancient Greeks were rather superstitious. They needed the protection of the gods to sail these waters. A number of temples and altars were spread along the steep coastline.

There was the belief that the Cyanean rocks (the Symplegates) with their blue-green copper tinge, at the very end of the Bosphorus Straits used to perpetually clash into one another not allowing anybody coming from the *Propontis* (the Sea of Marmara) to sail into the *Pontus* (the Black Sea). This shows the fears they had at that time, sailing up North into what they called Pontus *Aieuxinos* – inhospitable sea.

The Argonauts were said to have come this way to get to Cholchis in search of the Golden Fleece. More likely they were just explorers, cruising the seas in search of new lands.

Nike tried to imagine the majestic ship Argo sailing by with Jason standing proudly on deck. The legend said, that before venturing to pass between the Symplegates, following the advice he was given, he let a dove to fly ahead; the dove got to the other side unscathed with only the loss of a feather or two and so the ship followed suit and got successfully on the other side of the two massive rocks just in time before they clashed together but then opened for the last time never to move again.

The *Pontus* then became *Euxinos* (hospitable), an important trade route ever since. Standing there in awe, Nike could almost believe the story. The whole place was somewhat eerie, with a thick mist sweeping over the rocks, barely visible in the distance.

And yet it was such an exhilarating moment to see what none of her contemporaries ever could: those impressive straits centuries before the great city of Constantine was built.

There was already a Greek settlement there, on the other side of the gulf to where they were standing, called Byzantium, which Seuthes told her owed its existence to its unparalleled location for trapping tuna, migrating from the Pontus to the Mediterranean.

An active grain trade was flourishing too; the main stage on the so-called "corn route", for the Athenians depended on supplies of corn from the area around *Bosphorus Cimmerius* (present day Crimea, the straits connecting the Black sea and the Sea of Azov).

"They say, that when his oracle at Delphi was questioned," Seuthes explained, "Apollo had advised on building a new city opposite of the "city of the blind"(you know, the oracle of Delphi is known for giving particularly ambiguous answers); but at any rate the latter simply had to be the city of Chalcedon on the opposite (Asian) side of the Bosphorus, that had been founded some years earlier by the Megarians who overlooked the much superior site.

The locations might seem equally convenient, but in fact it is very difficult to sail to Chalcedon because the current will take you to Byzantium even if you do not wish it; if you want to cross from Chalcedon to Byzantium you can't go straight across, you have to go to Chrysopolis first and then drift down with the current which carries you there.

And another thing - the harbour of Byzantium is a lot better because it's deep and well sheltered. It's no surprise that with these advantages it's called *Chrysoceras* - The Golden Horn.

And don't forget the fish; this is the side they come to. The tuna just rush into those gulfs close to the walls of Byzantium and are easily caught. They don't care for the Chalcedonian shore at all."

The city of Byzantium was a stronghold, protected by high walls. An Acropolis of a sort was erected at the highest point as an indication of its glorious future.

Nike pointed out that this was a town very well placed strategically and asked Seuthes whether he did not find it an ideal spot for the ultimate impregnable fortress that one could think of.

"Oh, yes, you are absolutely right, that's quite the place for a fortification. However it's situated at a crossroads and it's completely exposed and unprotected landward. It's no good announcing to the rest of the world where exactly you are. It's not our way at any rate. We like to move about, to stay here and there, what's the point of getting too settled, too well established?

Besides, even the Athenians were not able to keep Byzantium. It's presently in the hands of the Lacedaemonians. The fortunes of war, you see change all the time. Clearchus, son of Rhamphias is now the governor of the city and I am afraid he is not a friend of mine. So we are not going to be made welcome there."

"He is right," thought Nike. "Invincible as it might seem, Byzantium, by then called Constantinople, fell to the Ottoman Turks, albeit after a lengthy siege."

"You have a point there," she said aloud.

"In order to be so bold," Seuthes was saying, "you have to have a considerable force to back you up, in case of an attack or siege and there needs to be a lot at stake to make it worth your while. Remember Troy. Everybody said it was unassailable and yet, the Greeks razed it to the ground."

"You say that as if you've been there!" exclaimed Nike.

"I might not have been, but my ancestors were. At least that's what I've heard from my father. That's the story that has been passed down in the family. Our people were allied with the Trojans; they fought valiantly side by side with them. The great king Rhesus, our leader, was slain there."

"Homer mentions him in his "Iliad". He was wearing this shining armour…What were the lines? "A marvel to behold, such armour is more fitting for immortal gods than for mortal men to wear…""

"Homer? Maybe. But we have our own songs and tales to remind us of those times."

"Fascinating," said Nike to herself. "At least we are getting somewhere; he reckons that the Trojan War really did take place; more to the point it all happened some time ago - a century or two? That's difficult to say, because it's so confusing, they have a completely different way to measure the passing of time!

The trouble is when one studies ancient history a century or two doesn't make much odds, it's all so long ago, but when you are in the thick of it, it suddenly takes on a much greater importance."

ALCIBIADES

Her attention so taken, Nike had not noticed the envoy just arrived, seeking an audience with Seuthes. He appeared to be very excited by the news he had learnt.

"Well, well, well as I was saying the fortunes of war change all the time. What do you know! While we've been happily journeying along, events have been happening not so far away. Our friend Alcibiades has just won a naval battle at Cyzicus and is very pleased with himself. And the Lacedaemonians sent an embassy to Athens and are suing for peace.

But Alcibiades, what a man! Charismatic but such a great strategist too! Exactly when things were going badly for the Athenians, he manages to turn the tide in their favour. We'll pay him a visit. It's getting interesting, Nike!"

"Alcibiades? Who's he?"

"Oh, you must know him, everybody does. Especially the ladies. Now there is a lady's man par excellence!"

The name sounded vaguely familiar. He must be one of the Athenian commanders. But Seuthes continued excitedly:

"There is a lot to say about Alcibiades, just a few words won't suffice. He is handsome, unruly, unpredictable and brilliant. An orphan, he was brought up by Pericles, who was his relation. Close friend of Socrates that you are so enthusiastic about. I think they saved each others lives during the war.

Very brave Alcibiades is, to the point of recklessness. They blamed him for the destruction of the *hermai* in Athens just on the eve of the Sicilian expedition which turned into a disaster."

"The *hermai* ?"

"Monuments of Hermes, you know. This was seen as a serious crime and a bad omen for the outcome of the expedition he was leading. And Hermes didn't favour him. So he defected to the Lacedaemonians. But would he behave sensibly there? Not Alcibiades.

He got involved with the wife of the king, Agis II, got her in a certain way actually. So he had to run away again! This time to Persia, to Tissaphernes himself, the same who's been financially supporting the Peloponnesian fleet. A master of trickery, Alcibiades won the admiration of this satrap and tried to use his influence to favour his compatriots. He's been playing one against the other ever since.

Eventually the new Athenian government, the so called "five hundred" recalled him and reinstated him as an Athenian general. He seriously upset the Persians during the battle of Abydos, the main naval base of the Peloponnesians, but at least the Athenians forgave him his previous treachery, for he arrived just in time with reinforcements to tip the scales in their favour.

And now this is his moment – with a victory at Cyzicus, he is back in the game again. He wants a favour from me it seems and I can guess what he wants me to do."

A boat took them from the harbour of Selymbria (a fortified town built on a rather steep hill, just west of Byzantium) to the camp of Alcibiades at Cyzicus. Seuthes left most of his people in Selymbria, taking only about a dozen with him plus Nike to meet the general.

She was enthralled by Alcibiades from the first moment. Such a charming man, with such pleasing manners! And yet there was something about him she did not like. Perhaps the way he was looking at her; she felt almost naked under his gaze and she blushed, something that hadn't happened to her for a very long time.

They were reclining on their left sides on couches, as is the Greek way, drinking wine and having a light conversation which gradually became more and more involved.

The wine had been diluted with water in a *krater* (a large mixing bowl), for any other way of drinking it was considered barbaric by the Athenians, a slave had ladled the wine into the *oinochoe* (jug), ready to be poured into each cup in turn. The cups were appropriately decorated with images of men, reclining and drinking from decorated cups. Wonderful!

"Now is the moment to finish them off," Alcibiades was saying, "but you know how it is in Athens. They might agree on a peace treaty, which would be silly because it would just give time to the Lacedaemonians to rebuild their fleet again. We need to regain Byzantium and with it mastery over the Propontis and the Bosphorus. And you can help me there, Seuthes. With your land forces from one side and my fleet from the other..."

"It won't be that difficult," agreed Seuthes. "Clearchus is a good commander, but I hear he hasn't made a lot of friends in Byzantium."

"Hasn't he?"

"Apparently he's been enforcing a very harsh discipline there; you know the Spartan ways, no doubt. The locals are not very pleased with that. So with inside help this affair can be organised very neatly."

Later, back in their camp at Selymbria, Nike said to Seuthes: "I don't trust the man, pleasant as he is."

Seuthes shrugged his shoulders:

"Neither do I. He's just looking after his own interests. We'll be looking after ours. But he is right. They have to press home their advantage and retake Byzantium.

He obviously needs money and assistance to achieve his ends. Are the Athenians going to agree with him? He reckons they might sign a peace treaty. Somehow I don't think they'll do that. I am sure he doesn't think that either. No matter what he is saying. But he wants to press on because time is precious.

They'll ponder over it in Athens. But at the moment they feel stronger and they'll eventually decide to keep on fighting. But by the time they reach that conclusion, it might be too late, they might lose their advantage.

Anyway, I promised him I would be ready and if necessary, I'll assist him. But we'll see. We'll carry on and I'll talk to my allies round here."

Next stop along the coast of Propontis (now the Sea of Marmara) was the Thracian city of Rhaedestus, situated at the foothills of the sacred mountain Hiron Oros or Kogainon as they called it, which encircled its picturesque bay.

The Great Mother Goddess was identified with the majestic mountain with the little city nestling in her embrace, an allusion to the way the Goddess enfolds her lover. Indeed it appeared in a way to be a sacred centre of the kingdom.

For the Thracians the Great Mother Goddess was a personification of the Universe (Earth). She conceived on her own and gave birth to a son (representing heaven, sun, fire) with whom she then mated and gave birth to another son, born when the rays of the sun touched her (either at sunrise or sunset). Her son was represented by a bull that was slaughtered; his blood soaked the Earth and got her pregnant. The son was reborn as the Sun God. This strange story in a way illustrates the cyclical nature of life: birth-death-rebirth etc.

Nike gathered that some mysterious rituals possibly representing this myth were performed there in the caves at certain times of the year and were connected of course with fertility. And there was a rumour that the royal treasures were buried here too. Nike didn't have the chance to question Seuthes on these and other topics of interest, for he was busy talking to the local dignitaries who had come to meet them, then they were whisked away for the customary banquet and after the amount of drinking they did, she had other things in mind.

HELLESPONT

They continued their journey along the Thracian *Chersonese*, the coast of the *Propontis* through Gallipoli in the direction of Hellespont, another place of interest for Nike.

Seuthes pointed out to her Mount Olympus, very far away to the west, covered with snow and she tried to see in her mind's eye the gods who were believed to live there. But viewing the summit covered as it was by year-round snow, she somehow did not think it a suitable place for anybody to live, let alone the Greek gods; and all that about having the place air-conditioned seemed rather far fetched.

She decided at that rate she would have favoured Everest if she were in their shoes, it was at least higher and more spectacular. But each to their own.

Nike asked Seuthes if he had ever been to Greece and was surprised when he replied affirmatively. He'd spent time in Athens some years ago and what is more he was made an honorary Athenian citizen. It was there that he met Callias and became friends with him.

Meanwhile they continued their journey south into *Chersonese* (present day Gallipoli in Turkey). Finally they reached a point where Europe and Asia Minor were separated only by a narrow sea channel.

They surveyed the narrowest part between the cities of Sestos and Abydus and Nike wandered if this was the place where Leander had ventured to swim the stormy sea to get to his beloved Hero, the priestess of Aphrodite; it wasn't at all surprising that he was drowned and driven by despair, she also cast herself into those unforgiving waters. A poignant story!

No doubt Lord Byron thought so for he had swum across the very same straits too, following Leander's example...

Somewhere around here also would have been the grave of Helle who, riding behind her brother Phrixus on the flying Golden Ram when they fled from their wicked step-mother, had unfortunately lost her grip and consequently her life, giving her name to the Straits where she drowned - Hellespont; a lot more fitting and romantic one than Dardanelle, its present (or rather future) name.

Nike had always felt sorry for poor Helle. Why was it that she had to die so young, while her brother was the lucky one to survive the incredible flight from Hellas to Colchis (reckoned to be in present day Georgia on the Black Sea), to be accepted into the royal family there and to live happily ever after? It did not seem fair somehow.

According to some accounts Helle didn't actually die but was transformed into a sea goddess by Poseidon himself, but even so it was a sacrifice of this young life.

The Golden Ram, their only means of escape was also sacrificed to the gods and it was precisely its fleece the Argonauts were searching for in the north. But one should not take these myths too seriously! The truth was surely a lot simpler.

The Argonauts were most likely adventurers, who were not chasing after rainbows, but exploring the unknown waters of the Pontus and if they found riches during their voyage, so much the better for them!

Seuthes was not thinking about Helle or the Argonauts at this moment. More recent events were on his mind. Hellespont was the place where Xerxes, the king of Persia had crossed to Europe, his people having constructed a pontoon made of boats turned upside down; from this point he proceeded westwards to fight the Greeks; he succeeded to sack Athens but was eventually expulsed and returned to Persepolis in Persia.

These events took place about 70 years ago. A time when the great Thracian king Teres was building the foundations of his kingdom; a mighty kingdom that Seuthes had inherited and held dear; a kingdom that he fervently hoped would endure and prayed the gods to protect.

Seeing the tense expression on Seuthes' face, it suddenly dawned on Nike that not only was this spot connected with mythological characters. Bloody battles had also taken place here; and not just those still to come in the 20th century.

Nike remembered "the grain route", mentioned by Seuthes earlier and then another recollection came back to her: of course! The Athenians might be smug about Alcibiades' victory as much as they like, but their luck was not going to last long.

The Peloponnesian war ends with the victory of the Spartans exactly here, at Hellespont; an event that brought to a halt the "grain route" and brought the Athenians to their knees, because they absolutely depended on it for their supply (grain being the staple diet). Not to mention that their fleet had in turn been entirely destroyed!

Reaching the end of the channel, our travellers stood to admire the view. On one side the Aegean Sea stretched out before their eyes; while on the other, they were able to observe Asia Minor.

Seuthes pointed towards Mount Ida, in the foothills of which was situated ancient Troy. The Greek camp would have been spread out along the beach before it. Somewhere around there Achilles would have been sulking, Agamemnon would have been planning his strategic moves, Odysseus contemplating his wooden horse.

There was another town in its place now; which was not surprising, it followed from what the archaeologists had discovered. They had found quite a few cities built one on top of the other; Homer's Troy was supposed to be the 6th out of nine altogether; the 9th being the Roman city of *Novum Ilium*.

Wasn't Constantine the Great thinking of founding his capital there? Nike wrinkled her eyebrows trying to remember what she had read on this topic. It was probably an idea inspired by the supposed connection between the great Troy and Rome.

That was it; the "Aenid" by Virgil was a celebrated work in Rome at the time; the story of the Trojan hero Aeneus escaping by a miracle from the burning Troy, whose descendant, Romulus, founded a new city, Rome.

It was entirely possible that Constantine would consider going back to the source so to speak, to make a fresh start. But his ultimate choice was far better. And his city still exists, albeit under the name of Istanbul, after having changed hands so often.

Nike was reflective. A visit to such places always starts you thinking on a broader scale and somehow helps you to put things into perspective.

The news about the rejection of the peace offer eventually reached them. Seuthes had been spot on with his assumptions. It was Callias in person who brought the news; he had heard that Seuthes was in the area and had come to see him. Nike, who had been curious about him for so long, liked Callias very much. He wasn't particularly attractive, neither had he the suave manners of Alcibiades. What he did have was a very appealing, yet slightly mischievous smile and a reassuring presence.

They discussed the present state of affairs with him. Callias said that there had been great rejoicing in Athens at the news of the victory at Cyzicus and many Athenians badly wanted peace; he being one of them. But others thought differently; that they were now the superior force and should continue to the bitter end. Their views had prevailed.

Callias reckoned that the Athenians weren't going to waste their present advantage. They wanted a more decisive victory. They were planning to fortify the town of Chrysopolis in Asia

Minor situated just opposite Byzantium and then attempt to regain the latter, which actually did not happen for another 2 years, but of course they couldn't have known it at the time. Neither had they any idea how long the war was going to continue.

Nike decided to keep her mouth shut; a wise decision. The fate of the Trojan princess Cassandra, whose predictions, concerning the fall of Troy, nobody believed, had to be a fair warning. How could she possibly tell Seuthes and Callias that everything was going to be in vain: the Athenians should've accepted that peace offer, for years of war still lay ahead and the final victory was going to be for the Lacedaemonians! All this was still to come. And if you ever have some glimpse into the future, you should know better than to try to use it to change destiny.

Callias did not stay with them long, he had to press on and Seuthes saw him off with certain regret. Just then came a dispatch from Alcibiades. He was calling off the plan for the joint offensive. Seuthes was rather disappointed:

"He's got cold feet. I don't blame him though. With Athens still on the go he does not need me at the moment. He doesn't want me involved unless he has no other option. But he wishes to keep me in reserve; one cannot be too careful, besides he has a couple of castles around here and he intends to hold on to them. Then again you never know, we might still do some fighting on Athens behalf."

But this last remark was made without real conviction.

THE TEMPLE OF DIONYSUS

On the way back they followed the course of the river Hebrus stopping at various residences on their route. At one point they turned westwards into the mountains.

Seuthes announced that they would be going to the Dionysus Temple to consult the oracle. Nike was surprised for there were temples of Dionysus all over the place, what was so special about this one? Seeing the blank look on her face, Seuthes expressed his astonishment at her ignorance.

Apparently it was as famous as Apollo's Temple in Delphi, famed not only for the temple itself but also for the predictions made by its Prophetess. He also told her that priests from the Bessoi tribe were the guardians of the Sacred Temple and he had already sent word of his intentions.

They travelled for sometime through a dense wooded area. The trail was getting quite steep. When eventually they came out to a clearing, it was twilight and Nike beheld in amazement a magnificent structure entirely cut into the rocks just above them on the bare stony hilltop. This was the Temple reaching for the stars, on the very peak, built of massive boulders. It was really a stunning view, this enormous building so sumptuously decorated.

A road carved into the rocks led towards it. It was paved with huge blocks of stone and they were headed for it. The road was enclosed on both sides by walls of rock and Nike felt somewhat hemmed in. Then suddenly they reached the end of this rock corridor and the Temple rose in front of them in all its splendour.

Seuthes left his men to wait outside and ushered Nike inside the Temple. They walked in silence, Seuthes lost in thought, Nike rather intimidated, until they entered a vast oval hall, entirely open to the sky, which was clear that night so the constellations were visible, notably Orion. There was a round altar in the centre, raised about 10 feet above the floor on a stone platform.

Nike looked around her with interest.

"Why isn't there any roof?" asked Nike.

Seuthes looked at her surprised:

"To be able to appeal to the sun Apollo when he is in the upper hemisphere, i.e. in day time, and Dionysus when he is in the lower hemisphere, i.e. at night."

They were expected. The Sibyl herself came towards them, a small bony figure with piercing eyes. A quick discourse followed, from which Nike did not comprehend a word. Finally they approached the altar and looked at the fire burning there.

At Seuthes' bidding, the Prophetess performed the customary ritual and poured libations into the fire. The flames rose towards the sky, but then shrank back, although still alight, under the defiant gaze of Orion, the great hunter, who dared to defy the gods.

The Prophetess and Seuthes were watching this dying fire for sometime. Then the Prophetess sighed and made a pronouncement. It was clear that Seuthes did not like what he heard. He raised a question to which the answer was negative. The Sibyl looked at Nike and that stare made her feel uncomfortable.

"You do not belong here," said the old woman in Greek.

Nike wanted to reply with something, but she could not even move her lips.

"She belongs with me," said Seuthes.

His face was grave when they took their leave. Nike did not dare to ask anything concerning the prophesy and he did not volunteer to tell her what he was cautioned about either.

That night they stayed in an accommodation situated in the Temple complex. Nike woke up with a start in the middle of the night. Seuthes was not there. It was quiet, but she could hear a slight murmur of voices in the distance.

She got up, wrapped Seuthes' cloak around her shoulders and tip-toed out of the room into a sort of gallery. Standing at the balustrade she could see a big gathering in the great hall down on the ground floor; a group of Odrysian men dressed in more sombre colours than usual. It was the sound of their voices that had awoken her.

Nike looked for Seuthes. She could not see him. But there was a man with a golden mask on his face. This stirred some memories...a dream she had had some time ago.

A smell of incense flooded her nostrils, she recoiled back and darkness descended on her. She woke up the next morning in bed with a headache and with not very clear recollections of the night before.

They continued their journey the following day without much ado. A much more sombre mood prevailed as they headed home. But Nike felt more cheerful as they approached their current residence in the outskirts of Beroe. Seuthes also seemed happier when they reached home and busied himself with state affairs.

Nike thought that apart from the last grim episode they had enjoyed a rather pleasant journey and even the weather had been kind to them, for it hardly ever rained.

THE INITIATION OF SARATOCOS

Another exciting event in their life was the initiation of Saratocos, a youngster from the royal family. From what Seuthes explained she understood that he was the son of one of his sisters.

The father of the boy had been a close friend of his and he had been killed defending Seuthes when they were attacked in an ambush some years ago. The mother had been given away in another marriage and Seuthes had brought up the boy as his own son. He was very fond of Saratocos, even more so than of his natural sons. But the boy was far from being spoilt.

Thracian kids in general knew their place and mostly kept out of the way. The girls enjoyed a carefree life till they were married off. The boys went through an initiation rite which varied depending on their rank.

Just like in myths and legends. Hercules had to perform the 12 labours, Perseus to cut off the head of the Gorgon, Theseus to slaughter the Minotaur. A prince of royal blood had to show his utmost courage before being accepted as an equal by the other men.

So Saratocos was taken on a hunting expedition to prove his worth. Hunting was a very popular past time for the knights and they were obviously successful judging from the amount of game they were bringing home. But in this instance the boy was to go barehanded and without any armour.

Later Seuthes described the hunt to her in detail. The young initiate had indeed succeeded to strangle his first wolf with his bare hands, so he was granted the right to wear armour and Seuthes was clearly very happy with the outcome. Saratocos had got some rather nasty wounds as a result of this challenge that he was very proud of and made sure that everybody saw them; it was amusing to observe him showing off.

Seuthes gave another feast to honour his young relative and the adolescent sat with the adults for the first time and was very pleased with it all. However something unpleasant occurred at the end of the evening. It seems that Theorus, one of the Athenians present was much taken by the beauty of young Saratocos, more than would please the boy.

Ancient Greek society tended to consider love between males as superior than the heterosexual variety, but Saratocos, being the typical Thracian adolescent, did not appreciate the compliment.

Nike was not looking in that direction, so she did not see exactly how it happened but during the pandemonium that ensued, she saw the Athenian retiring with a black eye and his friends making an official complaint to Seuthes. Seuthes took the side of his nephew and stated that such unwanted attention should not go unpunished. And the assailant got what he deserved.

Later that night Seuthes told Nike that this event was going to strain somewhat the relationship with the Athenians. But not even he realised to what extent.

The next morning Theorus was gone. And a couple of weeks later Seuthes received messengers. He was closeted with them for a few hours. But it was from the Athenians that Nike eventually heard the news.

"Now we know where Theorus went. We told Seuthes to apologise to him, but he wouldn't listen. Now let's see what he's going to do."

"But where is Theorus? What is he doing?" asked Nike.

The Athenians laughed.

"He is an impudent dog, Theorus is. But he is going to go places," replied one of them.

"Fancy that! He went to the Triballi and even now as we are talking he is planning his revenge."

"But how?" asked Nike.

"One of Satok's widows is now married to their king. Satok's son lives there too. And he is very keen to get back what his grandfather once owned - the rule of the Odrysian kingdom. The Triballi king is only too willing to oblige. There will be trouble ahead."

Fighting wild beasts was one thing but fighting the two-legged ones organised into armies, was quite another. Nike had felt secure until the moment the war started.

She had never experienced war at first-hand in her life. In her world wars always took place in far away countries and nobody she knew was ever involved in them in any way; her father did not do military service for it was terminated in the 50s, before he was due to be called up.

A war was always a nasty business even in those distant times when weapons of mass destruction were not yet invented. The present conflict was a dreadful awakening from her happy existence.

MUSTERING THE TROOPS

The wakening was as much literal as figurative, for a messenger was brought to her husband in the middle of the night with the news of the attack. Nike did not know how or where; in the commotion that followed, there was no time to waste in lengthy explanations. Orders were given and a meeting of the commanders was called there and then. Seuthes only told her that they would be going to battle shortly.

"But I knew it was coming," he said, "ever since we visited the Oracle in the Temple of Dionysus. Hard times lie ahead. But how glorious is to die in battle!"

He embraced her and held her close for a while. She clung to him, but soon he tenderly disentangled her arms and was gone. She heard him giving orders, servants were running about, there were comings and goings and the whole place was in uproar.

Nike knew at that point that her carefree life was at an end and her happiness would be short-lived.

The troops were gathered in the early morning. There was the infantry (known as the *peltasts* after their moon-shaped shields, *peltas*) they were armed with light weapons; and the cavalry, which was even more numerous; their magnificent horses trampling the ground with impatience!

The ones belonging to the royal guard had some very fancy harnesses heavily ornamented in gold and silver, and as for the knights' gear – it was beautifully decorated.

The war chariots were intended for the commanders. Seuthes' chariot was a masterpiece of gold and silver pulled by four horses; the charioteer barely managing to hold them back, such vigorous animals they were!

Seuthes was wearing exquisite golden armour with a golden

belt and a dagger at his side in a golden sheath; his cheek pieces richly decorated and ornamented with images of fighting heroes and his silver gilded shin-guards with strange representations of women's faces depicted on them, were flashing in the rising sun creating a sort of halo as if Candaon himself had descended from the heavens. He cut such a fine figure as he addressed his troops.

Nike did not understand much of what he was saying, but judging from the electrifying effect it had on his warriors, it was all very inspiring and he was greeted with ferocious chanting, shouts and brandishing of weapons.

She also experienced a surge of admiration and pride but at the same time she felt extremely agitated. Nike was concerned about her Thracian hero and feared she might lose him. Trumpets were sounded and off the warriors went to battle, led by the king.

Waiting for news is the worst part for those who are left behind and she had the impression that she had been pacing back and forth forever fearing the worst. That would not do. She felt so helpless, so useless! How would a Thracian woman behave? The Thracians relied on their gods for help; Nike would go and pray to Candaon, the god of war.

On her way out she inadvertently knocked down the silver jug bearing the image of the horrible winged goddess. She kicked it savagely aside.

Rushing to the stables, a thought struck her: she should make Candaon an offering. Something symbolic. The first thing that came to hand was a silver harness with images of Nike herself on it, which seemed appropriate. She hurried away to pray to the god for the victory of her people.

AN ENDING

They were victorious in the end, but what a price they paid! It seemed the battle had turned into whole scale slaughter. A large number of those mighty knights and brave soldiers never returned. Theorus and Satok's son were also killed. Her husband was brought back to her but she knew that he would not live long, so bad were his wounds.

Stretched on his back, his eyes staring at the ceiling, Seuthes did not show any interest in what was happening around him. Nike felt completely helpless and absolutely excluded from it all. There were all these people from their household in and out of the room with an air of purpose. Seuthes' bleeding wounds were dressed; one of his wives was wiping his forehead with a damp cloth, the other was directing the servants. They wiped the floor, which was covered with blood. He had lost much blood and was very pale.

Nike wanted to kiss him but with all that crowd around that was not possible. How much she wanted them out of there, how she yearned for a few private moments with her husband!

Towards the evening, torches were brought in and Seuthes showed some awareness of his surroundings. He wanted some water, but he could not quite drink it, it was spilling down his chest; it was terrible to watch.

Then looking towards Nike, he appeared to recognise her and to understand the silent plea in her eyes. So he motioned everybody out with a dismissive movement of his hand.

They all obediently filed out of the room, except for an old woman, who remained sitting in the corner. She was a servant and a very loyal one and had been with him since he was born. Nike had to tolerate her presence like it or not.

She did not know what to say or do, and moreover, this last

effort had exhausted Seuthes and he lay back on his bed, eyes closed, breathing heavily. She wiped his face with the damp cloth and moistened his parched lips. He opened his eyes and did not take them from her for a very long time. Nike pressed his hand to her heart and felt his ice-cold fingers responding with a last concentrated effort.

She hoped fervently that he would say something, but he did not have any strength left in his body. Soon afterwards he lost consciousness never to regain it again. Nike sat the whole night beside him holding his hand and praying for a miracle. At dawn she heard him fighting for breath. And then it was all over.

They dressed her in white clothes, the symbol of mourning; then strange rites were performed over a period of a couple of days, the meaning of which she did not know and did not wish to understand.

The successor of the king arrived, Nike knew him to be his eldest son Amadocus, and it was he who gave instructions for the burial. He was asking her questions, but she was not at all sure what it was all about and just wanted him to leave her alone. She nodded her head in approval of something that he suggested and he bowed as a sign of respect and left.

Now she could grieve undisturbed, she thought. But no, some time afterwards they escorted her out for the funeral procession. It was a poignant sight, everybody was in mourning, servants carrying gifts and even the fierce knights appeared to be saddened.

Heartbreaking music was playing and Nike started to sob again at the sight of Seuthes' chariot which was to take part in the procession; the white horse of the king followed behind the body, looking almost frightened by the proceedings…

They reached a huge mound with an entrance door, a monumental tomb, which apparently had been built well in advance. The procession stopped in front of it. A long passageway led them first to a rectangular antechamber.

The main burial chamber next to it was round with a decorated ceiling supported by a number of Doric columns and walls covered with ornate stone tiles. The body of Seuthes was placed there; a golden breastplate on his chest, attached to it was a silver plaque decorated with friezes of floral ornaments and both human and lion heads. A number of bronze vessels and the King's weapons were placed on the floor of the chamber.

Up to this point everything had been accomplished with no word or sound from the participants, only soothing music in the background. And then suddenly the sound of timpani clattered in and pandemonium completely ruined the decorum, all hell broke loose.

Nike was first startled and then terrified to see the other two wives of Seuthes, busy slaughtering his horse; blood was gushing out of the neck of this magnificent animal, splattering everybody around.

She shouted that someone should stop this madness, but her cry went unheeded and then she noticed a priest approaching her with a long golden needle in his hand and murder in his eye (at least she felt it to be so). Nike stepped back and he followed, she heard the final wheezing coming from the dying horse, there was that smell of burning incense in the air and…

Nike fell into a whirlpool of nothingness; she did not know whether she was already dead or still alive, she just had the sensation of falling…

Next thing she knew, she was standing in a circle of light and there was a man beside her, supporting her and holding a little box with some salts in it under her nose.

She heard him muttering something either to himself or to her, she was not at all sure.

"Am I dead?" she asked with a trembling voice, in English, for the elderly man holding her was clearly not a Thracian.

"Oh, no, no, dear me, no! Just an accident! Regrettably accidents do happen, I am very sorry to say! System failure, doesn't occur very often, but…"

"Please tell me what happened? Where am I? Am I dreaming? Or in hospital? What accident was that?"

"Oh, oh, calm down, miss! Everything is fine now! I've got everything under control. You are in a Temporal bubble at this moment, and then I'll be getting you to the tempo-lift which in turn is going to take you to your proper time. Don't you worry, everything will be well!"

Veronica rubbed her forehead to clear her thoughts. She didn't know at all what he was talking about:

"But what happened?"

"Bloody careless youngsters, that's what! Never taking any precautions! Screwed the temporal lift, that's what they did! And you happened to enter it from your century, which you shouldn't have been able to. What was the saying - "to be in the wrong place at the wrong time" - chances are 1:1 000 000 for such an event to occur, but there you go, it did!"

He shrugged his shoulders in an expressive manner:

"But all's well that ends well! It could've been worse! And the young idiots will be reprimanded, rest assured. Almost there now. Relax, take a deep breath…"

BACK

The rest of this strange encounter remained somewhat like a blur in her memory. She was gasping for air again. Somebody was dragging her somewhere. She was able to breathe easier.

"Seuthes! Thank God you're still alive!"

But opening her eyes Veronica saw another face. It took her some time to recognise in him Peter, the Bulgarian architect she had met some time ago…how long ago? She did not care to say – quite a few centuries ago.

"Peter!" she said. "What happened?"

"I've been really worried for you!" he replied. "What a silly thing to do – starting your car and not opening the garage door properly! You didn't want to kill yourself, did you?"

They were indeed in the basement of the building; she could see her parents' car in the garage, but Peter had switched the engine off. The garage door was now wide open.

Veronica recalled now her intention to go for a drive but lost in thought she must have forgotten to open the door properly (it was a heavy metal door requiring a real effort to move). Was she daydreaming again? She could not remember; it seemed so long ago. Or was it really?

"Shall I carry you upstairs?" asked Peter.

"Oh, no, that would be ridiculous!"

But the thought of the man who had carried her in his arms a little while ago and the sharp realisation that she had lost him forever, made her feel giddy. She leaned on Peter's arm and he escorted her to her parents flat. Happily they were out. Peter stayed with her for a while to make sure she was all right.

Veronica asked Peter to promise her never to tell her parents what had happened in the garage and wondered if she should tell him about her experiences. In the end she decided she could trust him and reveal her story to him.

It was the next day when she broached the subject as they were looking at the Roman ruins in the centre of the town. She started somewhat hesitantly, then unable to restrain herself poured it all out. Peter appeared very concerned. He led her to a park bench and questioned her carefully.

"I don't doubt your sincerity, but isn't it possible, for the sake of the argument let's accept that, isn't it just possible that it was some kind of hallucination, caused by the…"

"No, no, definitely not!" Veronica was adamant. "All that I experienced there was so clear, so vivid; I really did live in those times. Besides, how would you account for this, if it was all a mere hallucination?"

She handed him a golden ring, intricately shaped.

"It's an interesting object, I have to admit. Where did you get it from?"

"It was on my finger, when you found me. It was given to me by my husband, amongst other golden trinkets. I remember they placed it on my finger when we were about to join the funeral procession. I noticed last night when I was looking at it that there is an inscription, which wasn't there before. But I don't know what it means. You see, Greek letters are used, I can recognise them, though what they say makes no sense."

"Thracians did use Greek letters, because they didn't have an alphabet of their own. Which was a pity, of course, most of what we know about them is from Greek sources," explained Peter.

"I am well aware of that. I recall now seeing other inscriptions in Thracian on different objects. Greek letters were also used there."

"We could take this ring to a specialist. They could estimate the time it was made and try to decipher the writing," suggested

Peter.

"Oh, no I'm not giving my ring away! I'll never see it again! And it's all that's left to me from my Seuthes. And the dress of course."

"The dress?"

"I was wearing that dress, wasn't I? Didn't it strike you as being unusual for a dress? It is entirely hand made; hand woven and hand manufactured."

"Look, Veronica, I don't know anything about women's fashion, besides at that particular moment that would have been the last thing on my mind. But I'll take your word for it."

"So you should. Because I never had such a dress in my possession before I went back in time. Neither do I think you'll find any company that manufactures clothes like that.

I was wearing a completely different dress that day when I got in my parents' car. Wait a moment, I can show you some pictures on my camera, here, look. This dress is from a special collection, you'll not see every second woman wearing a similar garment, but never the less it's a style that you will recognise as modern, contemporary.

And now see on this other picture; I am wearing the dress I had on when you found me in the car. I took this picture afterwards and you can see the difference. What do you say? Do you still think it's a hallucination?"

"Yes, I suppose it looks unusual."

"It *is* unusual. It's a long *chiton* made out of very refined material, linen I'd guess or maybe hemp and it's white because white was the colour for funerals. I remember, I also had a golden wreath on my head, but it must've fallen off at some stage, so it's just the ring and the dress that remain.

But anyway, I'm not showing this dress to anybody either. Besides they'll start questioning me about the whole thing. I couldn't possibly tell them the story I've told you. Nobody will believe me. And my parents will find out, and, and…No, it's out of the question. But I wish there was a way to discover something more about that period!"

"Look, let's go to my place and make use of the Internet, if you want more information;" suggested Peter. "In the end I could tell you a lot about the Thracians but new discoveries are being made all the time and there has been a change in thought over what was previously accepted.

Anyway, what is certain is that they lived in these lands long before the Romans came, but you know this anyway, they left a lot of burial mounds all over the place, but especially in this area, archaeologists are actually doing quite a few excavations around here these days and are very excited by their finds; near by are the remains of the Thracian town of Seuthopolis, which are very well preserved…"

"Oh, can we go and see it? Please, please, can you take me there?"

But Peter shook his head:

"Unfortunately, that's impossible. The town lies underwater at the bottom of a huge reservoir. They found the ruins precisely when they were doing the excavations for the reservoir.

Nowadays enthusiasts want it uncovered and preserved and there are some rather daring plans like building a dam in the form of a well with the city on the bottom of it and what not, quite crazy and rather expensive. My father actually has a better and much more realistic plan involving scuba diving, but that's another story.

Anyway, Seuthopolis is very well documented. Experts say that it was rather like an ancient Greek town in its layout and surprisingly the royal palace was within the confines of the town, usually they had their palaces separately, away from other settlements."

"That's true," agreed Veronica. "The Palace we lived in was some distance away from the town of Beroe. A real fortress it was, they call it *poltyn*. It was always guarded. So it must've been another site all together. It's a pity though that we can't see this Seuthopolis place. Is it possible that it was called after him?"

"There were at least three Thracian kings called Seuthes; Seuthopolis was founded by the third one, I think. But if I can't show you those ruins I can at least take you to the Thracian Tomb at Kazanlak. They wouldn't let us in of course, because only specialists and VIPs are admitted, but still, for the tourists a full size replica has been built, a very good one I am told, all the murals can be examined and …We can go first thing tomorrow morning, what do you say?"

ON THE TRAIL OF THE THRACIANS

The rest of the day Veronica spent sitting next to Peter in front of his computer and sifting through heaps of information about the Thracians, which she found a very trying business. There were a lot of non-essential details and nothing of any real importance, as far as she was concerned. Peter remarked that she was getting rather obsessed about the whole thing and couldn't she ease up a bit.

"Of course I am stressed," she exclaimed. "Don't you understand? After all that has happened to me, isn't it natural? How can I live from now on if I can't discover at least some scrap of information about this past life of mine? I was there, or maybe it's more correct to say "then", whatever, I lived in that remote epoch, I loved and I was loved and I was bereaved and perhaps I was about to be sacrificed and all that happened in no more than a few minutes in real time. The time that elapsed here, I mean. I still can't digest it all.

You are the only one I've told about this experience, because everybody else will think I am deranged and perhaps send me to a shrink. And that is the last thing I need. You saved my life, Peter. Please, please have some more patience with me and help me!"

Peter took her hands in his.

"Just calm down, Veronica! I'll help as much as I can. I've already promised you that. It's flattering that you should choose me as your confident. And I'll keep it in secret, don't worry about that. Nobody is going to believe me in any case if I tell them your story. I wouldn't have believed it myself and yet, there is something about it and about you for that matter, that I cannot dismiss lightly. There, I am perfectly honest with you. But calm down and let's be more reasonable about the whole business."

"I'll try! Let's have another go and see if we can find something more on the Internet. The weird and wonderful things that crop up when you are looking for something! Wait! What are these?"

"These are *kukeri*. There exists an old custom, still followed in some rural areas of Bulgaria, where men dress up like the ones on the photo here and take part in a procession dancing through the village. It happens at the start of the year and before Lent. The scary masks, the bells hanging on their belts are to ward off evil spirits that allegedly had come in winter, and also to greet the coming of spring."

"But I've already seen a very similar group when I was riding with Seuthes one day!"

"It's not surprising; they say that's a custom dating from antiquity, it's got Thracian roots."

Veronica was intrigued:

"Who would've thought that it would survive to this day! It's amazing! But how come, this is a pagan ritual connected with Dionysus and Bulgaria is clearly a Christian country!"

"True, but lots of pagan rituals have been incorporated into Christianity when it was first established as a state religion. Don't tell me it's not the same in England?"

"I suppose there are certain traditions that were carried on...the holly and the ivy, kissing under the mistletoe at Christmas, dancing around the maypole and so on. You are right, Peter. What else do you think you've kept from Thracian times?

"Hmm, off the top of my head I'd say *Nestinarstvo* for example, that is dancing on the ashes of a fire in a state of trance," Peter replied.

"I've seen that too!"

"And *Trifon Zarezan* of course! On the face of it he is the Christian saint *Trifon* and his day is on the 1st February, but in fact because of his connection with vineyards and wine, he is none other than Dionysus himself!"

"Not Dionysus again!" exclaimed Veronica, "How fascinating! So how do they celebrate his day now?"

"Wow, drinking lots of wine as you can imagine. But you must be in the country where the vineyards are, to take part in the ritual. The viticulturist goes to his vineyard, turns to the east makes three times the sign of the cross (you see how its been camouflaged as a Christian ritual) and cuts three sticks off three different vine roots. He then pours some red wine, holy water and ashes kept from the fireplace at Christmas eve; this is all accompanied with blessings and wishes for a good year. The sticks cut from the vines are used to make little wreaths that they put on their hats or on the wine flask. There is a meal to follow, washed down with wine of course."

"Ah, that's not unlike pouring libations the way the ancients did. Not much change since, don't you agree?" Veronica remarked.

Later back in her parents flat, she had to put up with lots of jokes about her and Peter and had to seriously assure her parents that they were just friends that had a lot in common and that Peter had fuelled her interest in archaeology and was going to take her to some ruins and places, which in the end was not that far from the truth.

But Veronica found it rather trying to sit with her parents and talk about other things, like nothing had happened. From their point of view, nothing had changed. They were resuming a conversation from the previous day, when for Veronica that was a subject long since forgotten and in which she did not have even the slightest interest any more.

Her father would be asking for example when they were going to go to the mineral baths and she would be about to say "what baths?" but then would be checking herself and recalling the discussion they had had on the topic.

Next morning Peter appeared very excited and was being very mysterious about it, when he came to pick her up for their outing to Kazanlak. When they got into his car he produced a printout and asked her to read it and tell him what she thought about it. It was in English, from a Bulgarian Internet site and referred to a sensational discovery, made in recent years near a village in the district of Plovdiv, to the west of Stara Zagora.

A huge temple or tomb had been discovered of what was supposed to be of a mighty Thracian king, possibly Sitalkes. Other tombs were found in close proximity, thought to be of Sitalkes' brother and cousins.

"What do you think of it?" asked Peter.

But Veronica only shook her head wiping the tears that had appeared in her eyes.

"I've heard of that temple, of course," said Peter. "I remember when they discovered it because it was on the news, but I had forgotten the details. Sitalkes was his uncle, wasn't he? If I am not greatly mistaken, we can place him in the 5th century BC."

"5th century!" exclaimed Veronica, "So far back! So far back! And I was there!"

She was all tearful again a little bit later when they finally arrived in Kazanlak and entered the famous Thracian tomb. It was from a slightly later period, 4th Century BC and yet the whole atmosphere was so familiar to her. Veronica stood in silence for a while staring at the murals.

"They're so real," she said at length, pointing at the large fresco. "I remember grooms exactly like those, leading Seuthes' horses. As for those two, the lady of the house with her man, those two could very well be Seuthes and me, sitting down to a banquet, as we often did."

Veronica was sobbing now and Peter took her in his arms. He gave her a tissue to wipe her eyes and led her out into the sun.

They walked a little in the park and Veronica was explaining about the things she had seen in that past life of hers, as she referred to it. How the Thracian culture seemed so different from ours on the surface and yet if you thought about it more, it was not so very different at all. People had not changed a lot since then.

"It was such an eye-opener my stay there. Would you believe me if I tell you that so far back and they already had sewage systems?" she asked excitedly.

"A strange thing to take your attention," smiled Peter, "but I can well believe that, although you certainly wouldn't believe me, if I tell you that at the end of the 19th century when Sofia was liberated from the Ottomans, it had neither running water nor sewer system! Incredible, but however this much is clear from contemporary documents in the municipal planning archives. And Sofia has been a thriving town for about seven millennia; did you know it is one of the oldest cities in Europe? It definitely had all this in place in the Thracian period. As for Stara Zagora it was burned to the ground by the Ottomans altogether."

"Decline and Fall…"

"Yes, if you like. Or rather 'Rise and Fall'. The Thracians, the Macedonians, the Romans, the Byzantines and the Bulgars succeeded each other in these lands. What they built has endured. But there were others who left only destruction behind them after their raids. And the Ottomans. They demolished so much after they invaded the Peninsula; the only edifices they built which still remain are mosques. However like the Phoenix the towns of the Ancients are rising from the ashes…but anyway, you were saying?"

"Just reminiscing. A thought just came to my mind. He did tell me, that he went with his uncle to take part in the Peloponnesian War. That was in the 5th century BC, wasn't it? So it all fits together. The trouble is that there is so much that I cannot remember any more. It's so sad. I can't even picture very clearly in my mind the face of Seuthes…and I miss him so much! Couldn't we find at least his tomb, Peter? Maybe he lies in the same place as his uncle?"

"Maybe, Veronica, but we couldn't be sure. If it is not there, I don't think there is any chance to find it. Consider! There are probably more than 60 000 burial mounds in Thrace; it's physically impossible to locate the one Seuthes was buried in. Put it this way: the odds are extremely small. Besides lots of them were looted throughout the centuries. It's been a long time."

"Indeed. And I'll never see Seuthes again…"

"The Thracians believed in an afterlife," said Peter, "and who is to say there isn't?"

"Afterlife? Possibly. I accept the idea to an extent. And yet I wasn't prepared for there to be more deaths, more sacrificing taking place and slaughtering that horse took me aback, that's why I thought they were going to kill me too and I panicked. Maybe I was over-reacting."

"And maybe you were not. It's been said that they did sacrifice one of the wives during those funerals. Or rather that the wife would willingly want to follow her husband wherever he was going. This was supposed to be an honour."

"Oh, you are probably right! I never thought…but probably that's what Seuthes' son was trying to say to me just before…I didn't understand a thing! So it was like they were sending us away on a voyage, with the horse and the chariot and all, a distant voyage… how fascinating! And I refused to follow him. I wish I had known more about it beforehand, had been more prepared, more aware of what was going on! I just didn't have sufficient time to get used to their beliefs."

Veronica tried to pull herself together before resuming: "Would I have done otherwise if I'd known it though? I am not at all sure. In the end my ideas, my beliefs are from the present, from the 21st century. And I am not the suicidal type…and yet…"

"And yet if you could've seen death from their point of view, as the beginning of another journey, you would've gone with him, wouldn't you?"

"Yes!" And she was surprised at her own words.

Peter gave her a strange look and quickly changed the subject:

"By the way I forgot to tell you that I found out what that inscription on your ring means."

"You did! How come?"

"A similar inscription has been found on several vessels and another ring. It's said to have been "inconclusively deciphered", in other words they can only speculate, but they are not certain. The writing inscribed in Greek letters reads DADALEME, right? Which they deduce to be DA, DALE ME in Thracian, meaning "Protect me [Mother] Earth.""

"It's all clear then," said Veronica, "and you didn't tell me earlier because you didn't want to upset me more, not because you forgot. Don't deny it, Peter!"

She was pensive for a while and then she said:

"I would've liked to have a longer life with Seuthes. Back then I was so happy, so blissfully happy, I should've known that it couldn't last. You have it for a moment and then it's gone. I could've been more prepared to deal with the terrible blow that followed."

"But it's always like that in life, Veronica, isn't it? You are saying this with hindsight, but in the end you can never tell ahead of time what life has got in store for you. Besides you can't be sure about anything, can you? What happened to you might be seen from a different angle.

What if it wasn't exactly interference from the future, but something else – a near death experience, don't they use this term? I see, you've heard such stories. Isn't it possible that you had something like that during those few moments in the car, an encounter of a sort with the spirit or soul if you prefer, of this Thracian princess, who more likely than not did follow her husband into the afterlife but came back to haunt the places where she lived, crossed paths with you and recognising in you a sympathetic soul decided to share her story? Don't shake your head like that, it is possible!"

Veronica pressed his hand:

"Your English is improving very quickly, Peter! I wish I could learn some Bulgarian!"

"Oh, you don't want to do that! It's not a language you can easily pick up, besides only about eight million people speak it these days, so it's not worth the trouble. And it doesn't have a lot to do with the language Seuthes spoke. Or so I've been taught," he paused. "Although these days some new evidence has come to light (not that new actually for it dates from the beginning of the 20th century but was previously discredited for political reasons), which claims to prove that the Bulgarians are indeed the descendants of the ancient Thracians and Macedonians and so their language would not be that different, but I wouldn't know about that."

Peter paused again before continuing:

"History is written by the victor, isn't it? But I must admit it sounds very convincing and in any case there is no evidence that the Thracians were ever decimated. They had a semi-autonomous kingdom for awhile and when their last king died childless, he bequeathed his lands to the Emperor.

Those lands were incorporated into the Roman Empire and so the Thracians became Roman citizens, later Byzantine citizens. They were called *Vulgares* by the Romans/Byzantines because they spoke neither Latin, nor Greek, the languages of the "civilized". But of course this term did not have the same connotation in those times. From *Vulgares* came *Bulgares* and there you go.

Anyhow, funny you should mention the Bulgarian language.

It's a miracle that it has survived at all. It might sound simplistic, but I reckon it was because of the alphabet.

Unlike the Thracians, who used Greek letters for their writing, we had our own alphabet, purposefully created to suit our language, or any Slav language for that matter. The Russians use it as well, these days people even refer to it as the Russian alphabet, but it was created by two brothers from Thessalonica who are still venerated as saints.

It is said that their father was Greek, but their mother Bulgarian and so they felt very much for the Slavs who had to use the Greek or the Latin alphabet, neither of which was appropriate for their language. But it's a long story that every Bulgarian will be very keen to bore you with.

The point I am trying to make is that in the 9th century the Bulgarian king adopted their alphabet and made sure that it was taught in each and every corner of his kingdom. Literature flourished in that period and written records remaining from those times are still preserved; the language was so to speak reaffirmed and thanks to it, we survived as a nation even throughout five centuries of Ottoman rule.

Unlike the Bulgarians, the Thracians were assimilated by their conquerors a lot easier because they didn't particularly have written records and, in fact it was in their interest to learn Latin in order to be treated like all the other citizens of the Roman Empire.

There! Peter's little theory about languages and the role of the alphabet."

"It sounds fairly reasonable your theory, I have to admit," Veronica nodded in approval. "The Latin alphabet is not suitable for the English language either. In fact the famous Bernard Shaw, I see you know him, Bernard Shaw apparently held the same views and even used to joke that you could spell a word in all sorts of ways.

For example the word "fish" could be spelt as "ghoti" if we

take the "f" sound in the end of "cou*gh*", the "i" sound from "w*o*men", the "sh" sound in "revolu*ti*on" and you see, that gives you "ghoti".

He came up with a new alphabet, adapted especially for the English language, but of course people were far too set in their old ways, to be bothered with learning a new alphabet. Imagine the chaos that would have resulted if it were officially introduced.

Nonetheless, it's a pity. Anyway, you mentioned earlier, that you were taught differently about the Thracian language, but in what way?"

"It's a long story," Peter replied. "I was brought up, or rather my generation was brought up with the notion that the First Bulgarian Kingdom was founded in the 7th Century AD.

They taught us that these lands were inhabited by the Slavs who it seemed had managed somehow to exterminate the indigenous population (i.e. our brave Thracians, who were quite numerous if you care to remember what Herodotus had stated, that they were second in number only to the Indians)."

"Really? And what exactly did he say?" Veronica asked.

"Herodotus said that the Thracians were the biggest nation in the world, next to the Indians. If they were under one ruler, or united, they would, according to him, be invincible and the strongest nation on earth."

"Oh, I didn't know that!"

"Oh yes, it's true. Anyway. Let's return to the Slavs. So they had exterminated the Thracians somehow and settled down in their lands.

In the 7th century the Protobulgars came from the East, from Asia, a small horde of wild horsemen, nomads, but with a strong sense of how to organise and run a nation state and those horsemen of the east managed in turn to subjugate the formidable Slavs (perhaps after doing away with the brave

Thracians, the Slavs forgot how to wage war anymore, just turned to agriculture and decided to become non-violent and submissive?).

Whatever the reason, at least the Protobulgars succeeded easily to form an alliance with them, calling the new state after themselves, Bulgaria.

However they must have been quite overwhelmed by the sheer number of those local Slavs who actually assimilated their conquerors, and although they accepted Bulgaria as the name for their new state, they rejected the language itself – so, dismissed in such a callous fashion, the ancient Bulgarian language quietly vanished in the process – for present-day Bulgarian language is definitely a Slav Language, related to Serbian, and not an Asiatic one. Don't you find the whole thing preposterous!"

He smiled bitterly:

"But of course at the time we believed in those theories. They emerged in the beginning of the 20th Century, just after the Liberation from Ottoman rule. You know the Balkans were, and still are, notorious for their squabbles about all sorts of issues, territories etc.

Well, the West encouraged it at the time. There was a vested interest in having us squabble, to encourage the nationalists, to have us divided. Divide and rule, as they say.

If we laid a claim for all the territories our state used to own, there would have been trouble. So stating that the Bulgarians were late comers, that they arrived after the Greeks and the others, and that their State initially reached just from the Danube to the Balkan range, they hoped that they could get away with this.

And they did! According to a peace treaty, signed by the Great Powers of the time, present day Southern Bulgaria (where we are now), albeit with the status of an autonomous province, was supposed to remain under Ottoman dominion.

It took an ambitious Bulgarian monarch from the German Royal family to push things ahead and reunite the country at a later stage. Though his ambition led to other disasters. But that's another story.

And it was in those turbulent times that some people within Bulgarian scientific circles, perhaps paid by one or other of the Great Powers, suppressed the research of a Bulgarian historian, who found evidence that Bulgarians were living in these lands long before the 7th century, when allegedly the First Bulgarian state was founded. He maintains that those Bulgarians derive from the ancient Thracians.

"Thracians", as you well know, was a name given to a multitude of tribes inhabiting these lands, who had common language and customs. But they were also known under various other names, which were constantly changing with the times.

Some of them took the names of the territories they came from, or occupied, at that period; when they moved from one place to another sometimes they were given a new name, once they'd settled. But still these changes were not that dramatic. It's just rather confusing to keep track of all the migrations that took place at the time.

I used to believe that the ancient Thracians were gone, but not any more. They might have changed their name but they remained right here, where they belong."

"Fascinating!" exclaimed Veronica. "What a theory! But you are quite right. They could not have completely disappeared just like that."

Typing on the computer later that day, Peter whistled visibly impressed; he had found some relevant extracts from ancient historical documents.

"He was indeed fabulously rich your king Seuthes! They all agree on that one. Listen to this:

"His wealth (*dunamis*) amounting to four hundred *talents* per annum of money (*arguriou*) in both gold and silver, came from the tribute (*phoros*) from Hellenic colonies and Thracian cities, plus as much again in the form of gifts (*dora*) of gold and silver, besides woven and plain fabric and other accessories for him and the whole royal family."

Peter paused.

"Though what would 400 Athenian *talents* actually amount to in these times? Let's find out."

He was clearly enjoying himself.

"Here!

6 *obols* = 1 *drachma*

100 *drachmae* = 1 *mina*

60 *minae* = 1 *talent*

Minae and *talents* were actually never minted. We can see here only *tetradrachmae*, that is 4 *drachmae* coins from that period."

Veronica was looking at him patiently as he continued his search. She felt tired.

"Now look!" exclaimed Peter. "This is very interesting! They say that although it seems rather meaningless to compare it with modern currency, nevertheless, some historians and economists have estimated that the 5th century BC *drachma* had an approximate value of 25 dollars from the year 1990 AD! The wonders of modern science!"

"Really? Let me see!" Veronica said excitedly. "Have you got a calculator? Right! Let's see now:

400 *talents* = 24 000 *minae*

24 000 *minae* = 2 400 000 *drachmae*

2 400 000 *drachmae* x $25 = 60 000 000 US dollars!

Wow! That's the equivalent of what Seuthes was getting per annum just from taxes! The same again in presents and yet more on top! Gosh! Now I do understand what they were talking about! Indeed I knew that he was rich, but that goes way beyond anything I could've imagined!"

"I should write my memoirs," she was saying to Peter in the evening over a glass of homemade plum brandy, which cheered her up a bit, "while I still remember them...don't laugh, I could publish them as a historical work; why not? How many books do you know on this subject? You admitted yourself that the Thracians didn't have an alphabet of their own or indeed any literature for that matter, so they didn't leave any written account behind; what is written about them by the Greeks and the others, accurate as it might be, still remains subjective. What's more I have first-hand experience, who is better qualified than me?"

"Nobody, I suppose," replied Peter smiling. "You've been a contemporary! Besides they will name you along with Homer, you know, he mentioned the Thracians in his Iliad; they fought on the side of the Trojans; even some scientists reckon they were related, the Trojans and the Thracians I mean."

"So, it's settled then! I'll start my essay having Homer to compete with! But you have to help me, in the end Seuthes is one of your ancestors!"

"Oh, I don't know about that! You know lots of tribes crossed these lands; the Pelasgians, the Greeks and the Romans were here and the Macedonians and even the Celts at one stage..."

"The Celts? You are joking! Or perhaps you are not. Come to think about it they did get around pretty much all over Europe."

"Yes they did; they were here for a while – 60-70 years or so before they headed for the east (some of them settled in Asia Minor, others went up north along the Black Sea coast). Their capital Tile was not far away from Seuthopolis. So you see, you never know with all these mixed races (I don't believe in pure races anyway), he could've been your ancestor as well as mine!"

"Oh, no, God forbid! That would've been a very incestuous relationship, being married to my ancestor!"

"Don't let this worry you. Lots of unusual things happened to you recently, so one more, one less wouldn't matter that much."

"I need another drink after that! Have you got some more of this plum brandy?" Veronica proffered her empty glass.

"Yes, I'll have another one too. Cheers! It just occurred to me that here I am, having an informal chat with a Thracian princess, an old lady a couple of millennia of age, with a jealous husband, albeit some centuries back in time, but never the less still around somewhere, or sometime, and, you know, that's a scary thought! What if the boys screw up that time lift of theirs again and he comes back here to pick you up? I somehow don't think he will appreciate finding you unchaperoned in my flat having a drink tête-à-tête with me. He might decide to use this fancy dagger of his to see if I also have some blue blood in my veins!"

"He might. Or we might all go and try to prevent the Trojan War, who knows?"

"You do that! I'm convinced that if you were around when Paris was playing with the golden apple, Helen would not have been kidnapped in the first place and the Trojan War never would've happened!"

Veronica blushed under his eloquent glance.

"Life is full of wonders! Anything could happen on a night like this. Anyway. You are right, Peter. It's getting late; I am going to turn in."

A NEW BEGINNING?

She had a bad night, tossing and turning and she could not sleep, pondering over Peter's words: "If you've perceived death as the beginning of another journey, you would've followed him, wouldn't you?"

When she fell asleep eventually, Veronica had a bizarre dream. Or maybe a symbolic dream? Who knows? Anyway she was riding beside Seuthes in a chariot, as she had done so many times, but then there was a thunderstorm and when the sun reappeared she was sitting in a car, driven by Peter, just as she had been the day before, and then the faces of Peter and Seuthes were merging into one face and she woke up.

It was quite late in the morning, by the looks of it, so obviously she had overslept. Veronica tiptoed to the kitchen for a cup of coffee and she overheard her parents talking about her.

"In the end she deserved somebody nice to come along," her mother was saying.

"That James of hers has nothing about him at all. He is only interested in football and beer. I often wondered what she found in him," replied her father.

"To be fair, you are also keen on football and beer for that matter!"

"Yeah, but I don't go out to the pub every night to watch the matches with my mates, do I? And meanwhile our daughter was spending all her time in front of that computer of hers, was that normal? I know, she is into all that research, Roman civilisation and what have you, but I think she felt neglected. James didn't spend enough time with her. And her Internet surfing is pure escapism, that's what it is! I hope she won't go back to that waster!"

"This Peter is different, well educated, well spoken. Did you hear his father is also an architect? In fact he designed this very building," added her mother.

"Really?"

"Oh, yes. And a well known architect too. Lives in Sofia. Apparently there has been a restitution of land from which the mother benefited; she gave the building rights to a development firm and the father did the design; so they ended up with that flat up there and a couple of offices or something."

"Well, well, well…"

At this point Veronica decided to make her entry and the topic was not pursued further, but she was amused. There was her mother, not speaking a word of Bulgarian and already keeping up with the local gossip!

And Peter! Why hadn't he told her anything about it? She was impatient to go and see him, but then she thought better of it. He was busy. He had told her so. She would have to wait.

She pondered over it. Why was she so eager to go and talk to him? Was it just because he was the only one she could discuss Seuthes with, or because she enjoyed their conversations so much or was it that she just fancied him? She was determined to figure it out. And she needed some time.

Anyway her flight was due in a couple of days and she was already thinking of coming here again. And this time her parents were not the only consideration. She wanted to find out more about Seuthes and the others; about the exact site of his residence, the place where she had lived with him; about the other places they had been to; she wanted to trace every step they had made together and she knew it would be a lifetime's endeavour. She wanted to have Peter at her side but it was not fair, Peter had his own life to live.

"What is this?" asked Veronica, showing her parents a

photograph that she had just found.

"Why, that's the Thracian artefact," her mother said. "Don't you remember your father was telling you the other day that a few trinkets were found when the fence was put up. We took some pictures before taking them to the museum. I am still unsure what they are."

"And you found those in your garden?" asked Veronica incredulously.

"Why, yes. People do find such objects around here you know. The Thracians did live in these lands after all."

"I am well aware of that!"

"What's the matter? Are you alright?"

"Yes, yes, of course I am, but this has been so unexpected! Who would've thought? Those things are made of silver; displayed like an ornament on the riding tackle of a horse," Veronica bit her tongue so that she did not go on to add, "…a horse I knew pretty well and used to ride quite often."

"This is a representation of Nike, the Greek Goddess of victory," she added instead.

Veronica's parents were bewildered:

"How on Earth do you know all that?"

"How do I know? I just know it. I studied ancient history, didn't I? Take my word for it. These are silver appliqués, part of a harness."

"But they would look more fitting worn by a woman rather than a horse," countered her mother.

"Thracians loved their horses and wanted them adorned with ornaments no less than their wives. You have to take me to see them."

"They are in the local museum. I don't know if they are already displayed, but we'll find out I dare say."

Veronica went to her bedroom. She needed some time on her

own to think it over. Was it pure coincidence that this particular harness was found by her parents? She looked at the pictures again. It could have been a similar harness of course, not exactly the very same one that she knew. And yet, and yet, she had the feeling that it was the one.

She remembered clearly the day it was commissioned, her delight when she eventually saw the horse wearing it and her impression that Nike's face resembled her own, no doubt custom-made for Seuthes himself.

Was it likely that the craftsman might have produced more of these appliqués later? Questions, questions; it was like trying to fit the pieces of a puzzle. It seemed that everything happening to her was not accidental; it would be against all the odds if it were, was Veronica's conclusion, while thinking of the elderly gent from the future and the theory of coincidence he mentioned.

Peter and Veronica went for a stroll in the nearby Aiazmoto Park in the late afternoon. It had been a hot day, but the evening promised to be cool and fresh.

"I am going away soon," said Veronica. "You've been a good friend, Peter and I would like to thank you for everything."

"I wish we were more than just friends, Veronica, but the circumstances were not in my favour, I fear. It is not the most appropriate moment to tell you this, I know. But then, I might never meet you again; I might never have another chance.

I felt for you the moment I saw you standing in front of our building with your big suitcase, before you even spoke; I knew you were the one, I thought this is the girl I've been waiting for, she is coming into my life and everything will change…"

"Are you trying to propose to me, Peter?"

"I would, if I was confident that it was not going to be premature and ruin my chances. I could even go down on my knees if you would find it more romantic!"

"We could dispense with the kneeling bit. It's quite dusty around here. Besides it's rather old-fashioned. Seriously, Peter, give me some time, I have to come to terms with what has happened to me. I have to go back to Britain and settle my affairs there. But I intend to come here for Christmas and we can postpone this conversation till my return, all right?"

He drew her towards him and held her really close; they stood like that in silence for a while with the feeling that there were just the two of them for that moment in this golden afternoon.

It was Veronica who resumed their conversation.

"Besides, you need some time yourself to think this over. Are you sure, absolutely sure that that's what you really want? Aren't there a string of women somewhere out there," she gestured around them with a mischievous smile on her lips, "desperate for you, that you would rather be with?"

"No," said Peter simply, "I was too engrossed in my work of late to have any spare time for women. And yes I am sure that I want you."

"Didn't you feel lonely?"

"At times. But I am not exactly what you would call a "lady's man". I don't make friends easily and I tend to be loyal to the people I care for. Too much, I am afraid."

"You have been disappointed then?"

"Yes. You can say that. I don't know if I feel like talking about it at the moment. I think that I would need a strong drink before I could start on that track."

"I could do with a drink as well."

Later that evening, while sampling Peter's brandy again, he told her his story.

"It's quite banal really," he said ruefully. "Such things happen all the time. But I was young and impressionable. First year in University. I had a friend from High School; we were pretty close at the time. He had a younger sister; attractive girl, just a year younger than me. Nothing would've happened between us though, if circumstances didn't conspire against me (or maybe she had brought about these circumstances, who is to say). I was too much into my studies and very shy with girls.

One afternoon I went to see my friend, we had arranged to meet up at his house, but he wasn't there. The parents were out, at work, and Mariana, his sister, was on her own. She insisted that I come in and help her with her maths; she always had problems with her lessons.

So one thing led to another and we ended up in bed together by the end of that afternoon. Our relationship continued during the next year and my studies seriously suffered as a result, because she wanted to be with me every moment and I didn't have time to prepare for my exams, and they were particularly difficult that year.

We were to get married when I graduated and started my career. Then it so happened that her father got a job in the States. He went there first on his own and later the family followed him.

Mariana was very tearful on leaving, lamenting how could she possibly live away from me and I had to persuade her that it was for her own good etc. etc. We were constantly in touch to start with, then gradually we went through a cooling off period.

I was too busy with my studies, which I had previously neglected and I was extremely happy with what I was doing. But I was still looking forward to going to the States and to seeing her again during the summer holidays as had been previously decided. I had even booked my flight.

The time was approaching and although I hadn't had any recent communication from her, I just packed my bags and went to the airport. I was not worried, she knew the date of my arrival and we could discuss our relationship when I got there.

When I finally arrived, nobody was waiting for me and I was wondering what was happening, when her brother, my mate turned up. He looked somewhat embarrassed. When I asked where Mariana was, he replied that she was otherwise engaged and I would see her later.

Do you want some more brandy, by the way? Your glass is empty."

"OK."

"There. Anyway, when I eventually met Mariana she was very distant and aloof. She behaved like she hardly knew me at all. She was with some American friends of hers and she was only interested in them.

Then one of her friends, a big fat girl came to talk to me and wouldn't leave me alone; I overheard her saying to Mariana later "He is very cute, isn't he?" referring to me. At the time I didn't know what cute meant; my English back then was not good at all. Besides the jetlag had left me really tired and I must've looked quite dull.

Anyway, her friends gone, Mariana became chattier, but still not quite what she'd been towards me in the past. She wasn't interested at all in what I had to say about myself, she was just keen to tell me all about the exciting things that she'd done since she'd come to the States.

I felt rather hurt by her attitude and by the attitude of the whole family. They treated me as if I was some provincial guy, ignorant and simple, while they were so fashionable and sophisticated; their patronising behaviour really irritated me. I wondered how was I going to put up with it for almost three months!

I was to share a room with her brother for the family rented a three bedroom flat in the suburbs of Las Vegas. Later that evening when I was coming out of the bathroom, I bumped into

Mariana, who pulled me towards her bedroom. I was astonished by her change of attitude.

She closed the door behind my back and whispered: "You haven't kissed me properly yet!" I didn't know what to think really. I suppose with hindsight I should've asked her for the meaning of all that, but she was already unbuttoning my shirt and we ended up in her bed before I had the chance.

I hadn't been with another woman since she had gone away; I must've been really desperate at the time. Anyway at one point I disturbed a pack of photos, stacked on the night table, most of them of my Mariana, whom I had just been kissing passionately, snogging with another guy, or sitting on his lap or embracing him intimately. I was so shocked that I couldn't say anything for a minute or so. "I meant to tell you," whispered Mariana and the thing was she didn't seem very embarrassed, "I meant to tell you but, but…"

It turned out that she was planning to marry this guy, who was the boss of her father, a lot older than her, 15 years or so, but financially very well off, a big house with a swimming pool and what not. "But I still love you," said Mariana, "so we should enjoy the time we have together…"

That did it. I didn't wish to say anything to her, just got up, put on my clothes and walked out of the flat.

It was a hot night; I just wandered about reflecting on what to do next. I didn't have a lot of money on me. The trouble was that I couldn't exchange my ticket, it was a special offer and therefore with fixed dates on it. But I couldn't remain with Mariana and family either…

As luck had it, or fate? I had a very fortunate encounter just then. I ended up at a pizza delivery place and overheard two guys speaking Bulgarian. They were working there and got me a job - delivering pizzas, and I stayed with one of them in his apartment for the rest of my stay in America. We've been friends ever since.

There are kind people in this world, you don't meet them very often, but they do exist! You see, a pretty trivial experience, but it taught me a lesson or two about love, trust, loyalty and human nature in general.

So here I am 7-8 years later, allegedly a lot wiser, proposing marriage to a girl I hardly know and a foreigner in plus. And funnily enough I am sure that it's the right thing."

Veronica had tears in her eyes when she hugged him and whispered:

"I'm coming back, Peter, I promise. I just don't want to rush things, that's all. But I am going to come back and stay with you. And I need you so!"

ENGLAND, ENGLAND

True to her word Veronica was back in the beginning of December. She didn't regret her decision to leave Britain after all. Strange, she'd tried to persuade her parents to reconsider it at the time when they were about to move, then in turn her friends tried to discourage her from doing the same thing.

One of them told her, that she shouldn't rush into things; obviously she was still vulnerable after falling out with James and having another serious relationship with somebody else was not going to work; it was one of those affairs on the rebound and if she was going to go for it why get involved with a foreigner? Didn't she think it was risky?

Another said that it would ruin her career prospects; now was the time for her to press on and get it started before it was too late; squandering a year or two away without a clear career path wouldn't look well on her CV.

James' sister, Caroline, who came to see her, also expressed her disapproval; she was concerned about him and blamed Veronica. Apparently he was drinking a lot and he was down to the pub every night with his mates (he hadn't changed much then).

Caroline also had troubles of her own. She was pregnant and she wanted to keep the baby but wouldn't have anything to do with the father. Her parents were very upset about the whole business and she had had quite a row with them. At the moment she was sleeping in James' spare bedroom but didn't like it at all. Apparently he expected her to do the housework and she wouldn't have any of it.

"It's like a pig sty and I am not his bloody housekeeper, am I? Ordering me about like that! And I have this morning sickness too, which is made even worse with piles of dirty socks all over the place," Caroline wrinkled her nose in disgust. "You should come home and put things into some order. He wants you back really. He misses you. It would be great if you move back. We'll have loads of fun. You have to come with me on a shopping spree. I need some appropriate clothes, you see. People start to think I am overweight or something. In the end you are going to be the auntie, you have to give me some moral support!"

Veronica was listening to her chatting and thinking that the last thing she wanted was to get involved with James again. She had had enough of him.

Besides she didn't really like his sister. She believed Caroline to be rather spoilt and affected. Her babble irritated her but she tried to remain calm and not to show it.

"Why don't you talk to the father of your baby, Caroline? Don't you think he is entitled to know?"

But Caroline said she wasn't going to see him again, she wanted him out of her life.

"What I want is a make-over, she said, a new me so I can get on with my life. Don't you think I should have a new hairdo?"

She tossed her hair round to show off her highlights.

"It looks fine to me."

"Yes, but I'll go for some more outrageous colour this time, what do you say? It's all a question of how you want others to see you. My message has to be: I am a single mum, still young and gorgeous with a bubbly personality; and I want to have fun! I'll talk to my hairdresser about it all."

Finally Veronica got rid of her. She had enough on her plate to start worrying about Caroline or James for that matter.

On top of it all, Mandy, the friend she was staying with had a new man in her life and Veronica didn't get on with him at all. Phil was into interior design and he said that Mandy's house needed a makeover.

What's with people and makeovers these days? On one hand

there was this new trend to be green, on the other, everybody was more eager than ever to have their house gutted and transformed into a modern showroom-like home!

Anyway, Mandy was all excited and wouldn't be talked out of the idea; she gave Veronica an injured look at the mere suggestion to think it over before committing herself to extensive and, what appeared to Veronica to be, more or less unnecessary work.

Mandy didn't waste much time; soon after this talk, there were carpenters and other workmen about the place and Phil was giving instructions, discussing colour schemes with Mandy, comparing carpet samples or bathroom accessories and generally being in his element. The whole house was in uproar and there was no peace and quiet to be had; a peace and quiet which Veronica badly needed. She wanted to think things over.

Had she really lived amongst those Thracians of the past or was it just a dream? It certainly felt like a dream with the distance of time; leaning out of her PVC-framed window and surveying the very English, the very suburban, 21st century landscape, Veronica even wondered if she'd ever been away from this familiar place.

She wanted some advice from Mandy, but it seemed that Mandy was on a completely different wavelength. She was rushing about all absorbed in her new project and Veronica felt somehow she was in the way. And yet they had been so close in the past, discussing anything and everything and supporting each other in time of need.

Recently it seemed Mandy had changed; she wasn't the giggling, carefree girl any more. She had started to display all the concerns of a middle-aged woman. Or was it that Veronica herself had changed; after experiencing a life so different from anything she'd known before and which Mandy had not been part of and was not even aware of?

Whatever the reason, the friendship that had existed between them for so long had faded away and Veronica suddenly found it very difficult to have even the most ordinary chat with her friend. She started to go to the library and spent most of her time there, looking for all the available literature on the ancient Thracians.

Dinner time was particularly trying. Mandy and Phil would be discussing the new bath for example, which was to be a free standing one in the middle of the floor, and Veronica would say something about Roman baths and get a funny look from Phil.

"Really? Is that so?" would be his reply and he'd resume his previous line of thought.

Or even worse if she was explaining something about the renovations that her parents had done to their house in Bulgaria, he would come up with some very disparaging remarks or would say that had he been more interested in visiting that country he could've gone to see the house and given them some really cutting edge design ideas.

Once when Veronica was explaining that she preferred the climate in Bulgaria, he even interrupted her to say to Mandy:

"By the way, darling, have you seen my latest sketch for the hallway?"

And on another occasion:

"Really, Veronica, haven't you removed your stuff yet? I do need to get to the attic and have a good look around and it's all cluttered up with your junk."

Mandy tried to be consoling:

"You are welcome to stay as long as you want but could you put your stuff in the garden shed for the time being. It will be all right there."

Veronica had to grit her teeth and bear it all.

Later she overheard a conversation between these two:

"She doesn't give a toss that we've got all this work underway here, does she?"

That came from Phil.

"Well, usually she is more considerate, it's just that she didn't have the best of times recently; what with the job market being so bad and the lousy boyfriend she ended up with. I don't know what to make of it all; nothing seems to work for her. I reckon she doesn't give a good impression at interviews, doesn't appear motivated enough. And James wasn't exactly supportive either…"

"Ah, diddums! So she came to cry on your shoulder when it all went pear-shaped. And no sooner had you sorted her out, than she ran off to Mummy and Daddy and they managed to find her a new boyfriend! Blimey! She should get her act together, this girl, before it's too late. Trouble is she doesn't have a clue what she wants or what she needs."

Veronica ran away and didn't hear the reply:

"Still, I could hardly turn her out of the house, Phil. We've been friends since…since... forever. But the truth is – two's company, three's a crowd. I wouldn't mind seeing her go now."

Veronica was pleased to announce to them a couple of days later that she'd booked her flight to Sofia. Their reaction was not what she expected.

"So what, you decided to go through with it, eh?" said Phil.

"But why?" exclaimed Mandy. "Everything is going for you here, why bury yourself in that God forsaken place. Running away like that! Just because of this James business! You've been rather silly! Forget it! What? This Bulgarian guy, what was his name? But you hardly know him! You should've stayed a bit longer then, enjoyed your holiday romance with him and got him out of your system! That's what reasonable people do. We have all been there, we have all had our little flings every now and then, but there comes a time to act responsibly and put these things behind you."

"Instead of wasting your time with Thracians or Romans, you should put your efforts in finding a job and getting a place of your own!" added Phil.

"A job!" exclaimed Veronica. "What's the matter with our society? Why does life have to be centred on finding a job? Having a good job seems to be the one single most important issue for the vast majority. You are so smug about it. It identifies you as a person, doesn't it? It determines your place in society!"

"So what if it does?" replied Phil. "What's wrong with that? And you have to earn your bread, don't you?"

"True. But then if all those efforts earning money are with the sole intention to spend it on the latest models of the latest technical gadgets, which you hardly have any time to enjoy while lost in the world of work, what's the point of it?" Veronica smiled bitterly. "Some of the money you spend on leisure. You look forward to your annual two-week holiday, which is often disappointing, I bet. Usually herded to some holiday village or another, you might realise at one stage that it is just another adult version of a theme park. When I think of my last holiday to Ibiza with James, it was precisely that. I did not enjoy it." She shook her head. "No, no, money is not the be all and end all of everything. The Greek philosopher Socrates did not charge for his lessons. He was poor but he managed somehow and he was happy with his lot. What I am trying to say…"

"What are you trying to say?" Phil did not even make an effort to hide the contempt in his voice. "That you are like that darned Socrates and someone will care enough for your nonsense and let you teach them? Oh, get a life!"

Veronica looked at him and then at Mandy. She wondered what she had got in common with these two. This patronising attitude, these platitudes, this homely "wisdom" they were coming up with. What did they know about philosophy or about history for that matter? She mentally counted to ten before she replied:

"I have made up my mind. This matter is not open to discussion. Besides I am not going to encroach on you any longer…"

"But Veronica, it's just friendly advice! We do care for you, don't we, Phil? We want you to be happy. And you are going to make a very serious mistake, I'm sure."

"Maybe. But it's going to be my problem. Whatever the outcome, I have to cope with it myself." And she left the room.

At least her brother did not question her decision. She was very fond of him and it would have pained her deeply if he did. But then did he actually care one way or the other?

There was a big age difference between the two; he was about 15 years her senior and when he left home, Veronica was still a little girl. She hardly knew him, for he had emigrated to California and rarely came back to Britain. It was by chance that he stopped in London for a day on his way to the continent where he was going on business and invited Veronica for dinner.

It was a very grey day in November and she had been feeling quite depressed. His telephone call had come out of the blue in his typical style and had made her day.

She met him in the lobby of his hotel and they went to a fashionable restaurant not far from there. Oliver had a phlegmatic temperament and did not even bat an eyelid when she announced her news to him. He said he wanted to come and visit her there when she got settled, but admitted that he did not know anything about the country:

"Apart from the wine! I do like the Cabernet Sauvignon that comes from there!"

Veronica replied that she had learnt a lot about wines during her stay there and was looking forward to introducing him to some local varieties unknown outside the country. She almost added: "I've also tried a range absolutely unknown today," but changed it to: "wine producing has been traditional there since ancient times; probably that's where its roots are, in those lands."

"So, our parents have settled down there nicely, I take it?" continued Oliver. "But what about the political situation there? Is it stable enough, what do you reckon?"

"Oh, things have changed a lot since the Cold War," replied Veronica. "It is different now, democratic processes are taking place and even the King has come back."

"The King?"

"The former king; the country was a monarchy before, you know. The King is related to most of the Royal houses in Europe, including the Queen; he was an infant at the time when he was exiled by the communists. He has lived in Spain for most of his life. Now he is back home but not as a king, as a Prime Minister! No, I am not joking," she added. "He could have called a referendum, for the majority would have supported him, but no, he opted for a political career in which he had no experience whatsoever. There has been some disappointment. But never the less he is still quite popular."

"Wow! And you learned all that during your holiday there? What do we know? Don't make such a face! I still see you as the little girl you once were. You used to ask me to read you fairy tales."

"Yes and you always found an excuse why you couldn't."

"I was never into fairy tales, really. Science fiction was as far as I'd go; "Thunderbirds", "Captain Scarlet"…you wouldn't know them of course, you were not even born then."

"They were showing them again actually, not so long ago."

"Were they? It's strange to be back here again. It's almost as if nothing has changed."

"You don't really like it here, do you? Neither does Carrie. I wish I saw more of you two; and the kids."

"Oh well, you know how it is. I hope we'll be able to come and visit you in your new place before too long. Try the wine. Is it so superior to this Bordeaux here? You are not drinking. Cheers!"

Veronica also raised her glass and smiled to him:

"Cheers!"

But she was thinking that it was getting late, these few hours with Oliver had disappeared so quickly and when was she going to see him again; most likely not very soon, whatever he was saying, California was so far away and he was so busy and it was raining outside.

She would have stayed with him longer; going back to Mandy's and facing her friend and Phil, was the last thing she wanted at the moment, but Oliver had to get on an early flight; what with the jetlag and all, he did look tired.

Veronica noticed for the first time a few grey hairs showed at his temples, being so fair as he was made them difficult to spot and yet she noticed them, she noticed that her brother was getting older and sighed.

It was still raining when she got up the next morning and she felt she had to text Peter just to say that she missed him so much and she was counting the days.

Sending the message she thought it was a silly thing to do, Peter was probably busy, with the two hours time difference it was 10 o'clock there and he sometimes forgot to switch his mobile on, besides he wouldn't expect her to contact him till much later in the day as was her habit.

Hearing the warning signal for the incoming message she almost jumped. And there it appeared on the screen, Peter's reply. He was saying that he missed her too; he hadn't slept most of the night, he had just finished the project he was working on, he wanted to talk to her on the phone and when was the best time. These few lines, very ordinary otherwise, cheered her up.

Veronica was still in high spirits going downstairs for breakfast no matter that she almost tripped on Phil's trainers, spread across the landing and had to face the dark face of the latter who just glanced at her above his newspaper without as much as a greeting. She made herself coffee, took one of Mandy's magazines and busied herself with it.

"You have to move your car," said Phil eventually. "You are blocking me."

"I know," said Veronica. "It's not the end of the world, yesterday you were blocking me."

"So what? It's not the same. You are unemployed; you haven't got anything urgent to do. You could at least be more considerate." He went out of the room, leaving her to clear the table after him.

After days of rain, the sky cleared, the sun appeared and the world suddenly seemed a nicer place. Veronica had brought her horse to a standstill so she could admire the view. It was a perfect autumn day; the last of the glorious colours not entirely gone, a splash of reds, yellows and browns adorning the trees in a last hoorah, the last dazzling display before the advent of the grey winter, its coldness already in the air.

Veronica tried to imagine that she was back in ancient Thrace, but it just didn't feel the same. This was a different place, in a different time.

Down the hill the outlines of a familiar castle were visible, that was the residence of the Queen, Windsor Castle. It was peaceful around her, but Veronica could still see the white trails in the sky left by the planes making for Heathrow or taking off, hear the distant noise of the traffic from the road;

M25, 'the road to hell' was not far off.

Prior to her life in ancient Thrace, she had often wondered what it would be like without the cars, the traffic jams, the pollution, the noise. Especially without the noise. But she had never previously been able to truly appreciate what the words 'idyllic' or 'pastoral' meant until she actually experienced it.

She remembered how strange it was to look up and not to see or hear any planes in the sky, but just the birds singing; and the absolute sound of silence at night; not to have the concrete motorways and other structures disfiguring the face of Mother-Earth, but only dusty roads trodden by horsemen and beasts, their long empty stretches, connecting small villages hidden in the woods; peaceful scenes of shepherds out in the meadows grazing their herds, peasants ploughing the fields and vast forests extending as far as her eyes could see.

But here and now was another reality; it was for the time being at least, home, England in a 21st century autumn. Veronica was alone once again. Not entirely. Soon she would have to go back and spend another tense evening with Mandy and Phil. But in just a few more weeks she would be gone.

CHRISTMAS - PRESENT DAY THRACE

When she finally got on the plane for her flight to Sofia, she was really relieved to get away. She felt so tired! It had been quite a time! Veronica managed to dispose of most of her possessions. She had sold her car, her stereo and her TV set, most of her books, her CDs and other objects of any value. She had been to the charity shops as her parents had done earlier; she had given away lots of clothes and shoes (it is a wonder the amount of clothes and shoes a woman accumulates in a short space of time), some of them hardly worn.

Finally she sent a big box full of books and albums to Peter ("in the end," she thought, "this business might be costly, but I couldn't possibly throw these; my whole life is there"). So she had reduced her belongings to a bare minimum; packaged up and sent off only her most treasured possessions including those small trinkets that had great sentimental value to her.

To console herself, she recalled a quote by Jerome K. Jerome from his famous novel, along the lines that when sailing through life apart from the bare necessities, i.e. what one definitely couldn't do without, there is no need to burden oneself with anything else. So loaded with two big suitcases containing all her personal effects Veronica arrived in Sofia one winter afternoon to start a new life with Peter.

After the hectic time she had had in Britain in the last few months she just wanted to sit back and relax. In fact she had her laptop in front of her and was typing her Christmas letter.

Veronica always wrote a Christmas letter and sent a copy of it to all her friends together with the traditional card. This time she even included a photo which she had taken from her window; everything was covered with snow, presenting the perfect winter landscape.

The afternoon sun was flooding the room although outside

was freezing cold. She closed her eyes letting the last rays of the sun to caress her face.

As always she found it difficult to begin:

Stara Zagora, Bulgaria, 6 December

As you gather I've moved again! Seems I couldn't keep in one place very long or be separated from my parents! They are already installed in their new house in a picturesque village nearby, while I am about to settle down with my new boyfriend/fiancé Peter here in Stara Zagora.

Veronica leaned back in her chair and thought hard on her next line. Probably it had to be something along the lines "feeling at home here'; but it sounded rather tired; she could add in this instance "no wonder, I've been around these places since the 5th century BC", a private joke between her and Peter.

This was the trouble with such letters. She wanted to keep in touch with her friends, but while previously she would've been bursting to tell them all that had happened during the year, this time there was much more she would rather conceal.

Peter was the reason I came back here.

"I might've been dead if it wasn't for him. Following Seuthes on his journey, to the afterlife. Probably I wasn't meant to do so. I didn't belong there. Anyway, it's too late for that now."

He's an architect but his hobby is archaeology. He fired in me an interest in Ancient Thrace and thanks to him I am becoming quite an expert.

"He did start me on that track, didn't he? It was from him I heard the name of Beroe mentioned for the first time. Funny, he's actually born here, so is Seuthes, couple of millennia earlier. What would have become of Seuthes if he were born in our time? I could see him as a great political figure; I could see him as a leader of men today as he was then. He wouldn't be out of place now at all."

She imagined him with a mobile in his hand, dressed in a stylish grey suit and travelling in a chauffeur driven car and, strangely, it wasn't such an absurd thought after all.

"Time is such a good healer, I can think about him now without any pangs in my heart, I can even smile at such silly thoughts as that, Seuthes driving, Seuthes ringing me on my mobile, why not even Seuthes, the astronaut, flying to the Moon? I could see him being a hero in any case, any time! My hero! But that's enough daydreaming for today! Time to finish my letter!"

I am going to write a paper on this subject, having at my disposal all the research material I need.

"And more! The all important first hand experience; better than if I had been the special correspondent of such and such a newspaper or magazine"

I am also hoping to take part in some archaeological excavations in the New Year and am looking forward to that.

"I am not sure what I hope to find, probably my old pair of knickers somewhere in the archaeological strata; now that would indeed be an anachronism! Anyway it's going to be great fun!"

At the moment we are living in Peter's flat in Stara Zagora, but he promised to design a house in the countryside for me. Stara Zagora is a rather nice town, but these days I fancy more peace and quiet.

"I want to discover that corner, that place where I was so happy once-upon-a-time; if it's not already taken we'll go there; get away from the hustle and bustle, "away from the maddening crowd. This flat is all very nice, but it's his father's work. I want Peter to build us a new home, an exclusive place, custom made so to speak, to fit our lifestyle. The way I had those clothes specifically designed for me. I am still a day-dreamer am I not?"

So we'll keep you posted!

Have a very nice Christmas and a very Happy New Year!

There! She'd done it! Not a bad letter. Says enough, but nothing more. If she wrote everything she thought of, they'd think she was a raving lunatic.

Now she could turn her attention to other matters. Christmas. Wedding. They were planning to get married in spring. It would be symbolic in fact, a new beginning.

They had agreed that neither of them believed in long engagements. If you really want to spend the rest of your life with somebody, there is no point in putting it off. But now she should allow herself some respite. Peter would be coming back any moment now; they were going out for dinner. It was a nice and comforting thought.

Going to Sofia for New Years Eve was not exactly what Veronica wished for, but there was no way to decline an invitation from Peter's parents. They had just spent a quiet

Christmas day with her own parents in their new home and very nice it was too – exactly as she had imagined it at the time – a white Christmas and everything to go with it – the roast turkey, the crackers, the pudding and the presents under the Christmas tree.

She felt too snug for a trip to Sofia. Besides she didn't think much of the Bulgarian capital. True, she never had the chance to see it properly, but her first impression was not very promising; she found its urban landscape not particularly appealing, the potholes in the road intolerable and the number of stray dogs in the streets particularly disturbing.

Peter finally reconciled her to the idea, explaining that Sofia had a long history and was a thriving settlement in Thracian times. He then added:

"In Roman times it was called Serdica, due to the fact that it was founded by Thracians from the Serdoi tribe, the same way Paris owed its name to the Parisii tribe. Or was it the other way round?" He paused.

"Hmm… if I am not mistaken I read somewhere that actually the Serdoi tribe was called after the name of the town, because they say "serdica" originates from "centre" and indeed it's situated more or less in the centre of the Balkan Peninsula. The later name of Sofia - Sredets also deriving from our word for "centre", confirms that."

But Veronica wasn't listening anymore. At this point it suddenly dawned on her that she'd already been there in that previous life of hers. They had been on a visit to the king of the Serdoi back in the 5th century BC and that would have been his capital, though at the time it had another name.

She remembered clearly the mountain and some hot water springs and the young king and the admiration in his eyes (she had been very flattered by his attentions, but had felt that Seuthes was somewhat irritated).

The king of the Serdoi had pledged an oath of allegiance to

Seuthes and had offered him precious gifts. It all seemed so long ago now! And she was due to go back to the same place again and see it 25 centuries later!

"My Rome is Serdica!"

"Sorry?" Veronica was startled from her reverie.

"That's what Constantine the Great used to say. He loved the city of Serdica so much that he even considered moving his capital there. But as you know only too well, he settled for Byzantium in the end...Who knows what the history would have been if he had chosen Serdica!"

"You are joking!" Veronica exclaimed.

"No, I am not. Serdica was quite a city in those times."

"That's exciting. Let's go then!"

By taking the motorway their trip didn't last more than a couple of hours. Veronica was much more attentive on the approach this time. She scrutinized the landscape. There was Mount Vitosha, it was most striking in fact! How come she had not been aware of it before? It was the very landmark of the place, the only one that hadn't been altered by the ravages of time!

The capital of the young Serdoi king had long since been razed to the ground and his grave was lying forgotten who knows where.

She now saw Sofia with a different eye and realised how unfair she had been. For Sofia was quite a place, an attractive city not withstanding the disadvantages of any big city, traffic congestion, parking problems, pollution, crowds...and yet the traffic was flowing, the public transport seemed to be working and the air was fresh, coming directly from the mountain.

Peter had a little place of his own in the centre of town. His mother had been there to clean it prior to their arrival, because a cousin had stayed there for a time, but now he'd moved out to live with his girlfriend. Peter was pleased to have it back and he said he meant to keep it for their visits to Sofia.

"You know I have business here very often and I don't want to stay with my parents. They are wonderful people, but..."

"Yes, I know," replied Veronica, "parents!"

She made a face:

"Tell me about it!"

Peter was rummaging about the kitchen.

"There!" he was pleased. "My mother knows me so well! She hasn't forgotten to bring coffee and we could have some now! And plum jam! Yummy! Here is the cafetiere! You are having some?"

"What? Plum jam?"

"No, coffee," he proffered a packet of *Lavazza*. "What's the matter with plum jam? Don't you like it?"

"Of course I do! But not at the moment. A cup of coffee will do. With some biscuits."

"There aren't any. But my mother has left a box of chocolates instead. We could have the jam for breakfast tomorrow. It's home made by the way, I hope you don't mind that."

"Home made! Super! I haven't had homemade preserves since my Gran died. She used to make them."

"My mother still does. She'll give you some more, I bet! You can go to the front room and take a seat. I'll serve you the coffee."

"And the chocolates."

"Take the chocolates with you."

It was not a bad little flat. Peter had owned it since he was in his last year in University. It consisted of a room, a kitchen and a bathroom. The room was lined with shelves, piled high with books, files, reference material and goodness knows what else. Peter's architectural plans were all here. So too was his drawing board.

There was a certain charm to this den, but if she had the chance, Veronica would've changed a lot of things. But she didn't like the idea of living there. Not for a long period in any case. Peter said:

"That's because you are so used to all those castles of Seuthes. One gets used to luxury very easily."

"Oh, it's not that! You are teasing me, aren't you? What a thing to say! Of course that's not the reason! It's the noise, the pollution; I've never lived in the centre of a big town before. My parents had their house in the country to the west of London and I've lived there since I was born. Then I moved to Oxford. Nice town Oxford, it has such an atmosphere. But I had all that peace and quiet there too. And later on I moved in with James, out in the suburbs; granted it wasn't a paradise, but I had my own little garden and the neighbours were, on the whole, not bad. But here! This constant traffic! Don't they ever stop? And it's not even a main street."

"One gets used to it," said Peter.

But she didn't think she would. She was pleased that Peter didn't express a desire to remain here longer. True, the flat in Stara Zagora was also in the centre of town, but somehow it wasn't the same. They were higher up in their turret and besides Stara Zagora is a provincial town and does not compare with Sofia, no matter it's said to be amongst the top Ten Bulgarian Cities and is also a district centre.

Veronica actually enjoyed their stay in Sofia in the end. There was a certain ambience in the centre of Sofia, which she liked from the first day; besides, being based in the very centre gave them some advantages and she had to admit it.

They were able to walk here and there and didn't need a car, or even the use of public transport to get around; they would just go for a stroll along the yellow brick road; yes, as if by magic, all the way from the land of Oz, there was a yellow brick road in the centre of town; but one had to be careful in winter, for its surface was quite slippery.

Veronica and Peter went to the cinema a couple of times; she'd noticed they were showing an English film (with Bulgarian subtitles), the next show was just about to start and they went to see it there and then. They mostly ate out, taking advantage of the numerous restaurants in the neighbourhood.

The days that followed were exciting. Peter took her to the National History Museum, now located in a former government residence in the foothills of the mountain; just the place for the Thracian treasures, which are displayed there! But Veronica was also saddened at having to see these objects behind glass cases, after recalling Seuthes' people wearing similar jewellery and using such drinking vessels in their everyday life!

Some more collections were also on display in the Archaeological museum, located in the centre of town, in what used to be a Turkish mosque; however her interest was mostly taken by exhibits of the stone slabs with rare inscriptions on them.

"This weather is ideal for visiting museums!" remarked Veronica on leaving the Archaeological Museum. "It's so cold, I don't want to be outdoors for very long!"

"We'll just go to the Mineral Baths; you wanted to see the springs."

The Mineral Baths were not far away. The building was under reconstruction, and a bit of a mess, but in front of it a nice garden was laid out, now covered with snow, while a little further on were the springs. Peter was apologetic:

"They changed the layout completely and made a very poor job of it. People say they now look like public urinals and I quite agree with that!"

The small basins were lined up along low walls, forming geometric patterns and into these the hot water was freely flowing. There was also a little naked statue of a young Greek or Roman god, maybe Aesculapius, standing in the centre of a small fountain in which people had already started to throw coins. It's the same everywhere with coins and fountains!

The steam was rising from the hot water into the cold air. People were filling plastic bottles and even jerry-cans to take back home.

Peter bent down, stretched his hand under the water and drank out of the palm of his hand, but Veronica declined, saying that she didn't want to get her hands wet. Eventually under Peter's gentle persuasion she took a mouthful from his palm.

"It's quite hot!" she exclaimed.

"Oh, yes, 45C or more. These springs have been renowned since ancient times. A legend says that the daughter of the Great Byzantine Emperor Justinian (he was from Thracian origin by the way), came to take the waters, for she was suffering from poor health, and when she recovered, her father built a church and named it after her patron saint, St. Sofia. It's the oldest church in the city and also the one to give it its present name."

"How fascinating!" Veronica said, offering Peter a tissue to wipe his hands.

"Maybe it's just a legend, or maybe there is a grain of truth in it, who knows?"

"There is usually a grain of truth in any old myth or legend; at any rate it's a nice story. But it's me that could claim to have tried out these waters even before that princess. I definitely remember mineral springs, though everything looks so different now. If it wasn't for you I never would've thought that this was the same town!"

They had a candlelit dinner on New Year's Eve followed by the traditional cheese pastry containing little messages hidden in its layers, foretelling your luck for the year; not unlike the old English tradition of a coin in the plum pudding. Veronica's read "happiness" while Peter did get the coin, much to the envy of everybody present.

"One would think that it's a golden coin," joked Peter.

At 12 o'clock a bottle of champagne was opened and they watched the fireworks from the balcony. There was a certain enchantment to this winter night, at least for Veronica. When young, every now and then one is still able to perceive the world with a certain sense of wonder.

VARIOUS VISITS AND EVENTS

It wasn't until mid-summer, that Veronica had the chance to visit Sitalkes' Temple. She'd been too busy before settling into her new life. But time was passing quickly, doesn't it always? And by and by she reminded Peter of his promise to take her there.

Veronica had read a lot concerning the temple, about which archaeologists were so very excited. They said it was part of a Thracian cult centre, because they had excavated other structures in the area, including another temple, an observatory etc.

It was questionable though whether anybody was ever buried in this particular temple, allegedly connected with Sitalkes. There was speculation that such a powerful Thracian ruler was likely to have been deified after his death and that his tomb would then become a place of pilgrimage. Whatever the connection with Sitalkes was, the temple was built near a bizarre rock formation which was a site of religious significance dating from even earlier times.

Veronica did not know what to think about it all. She did recognise the temple when she saw the pictures. She had been there with Seuthes all those centuries ago. A religious ceremony of some sort was held there, but she could not clearly remember what it was. Could it have been in honour of Dionysus? Very likely. She remembered tasting the wine and apparently a winery was discovered adjoining the temple.

The Bulgarians had made numerous archaeological discoveries in recent times, which had not been widely publicised in the rest of the world, not in England in any case.

Veronica was overwhelmed by the amount of information found with Peter's help and which sadly she had not got round to analysing yet. She was very keen to go to some of those places such as Perperikon, Sveshtari, Tatul, to name just a few, and see for herself, but things were not that simple.

Peter had been very busy with work and she wanted to go with him on this "pilgrimage to her past" as she called it. Besides there were all these formalities connected with her moving to Bulgaria that had taken most of her time. Not to forget the wedding of course.

It was a small wedding, for most of her friends could not make it ("one would think that we live on the moon"), but at least her brother did come with his family and even spent a couple of weeks afterwards at the seaside! She had been very happy with it indeed; she knew Peter was happy too.

They had a civil wedding first and then a religious ceremony in the Orthodox Church, which was so wonderful! The wearing of the crowns, the candles, the choir, the saints depicted on the icons presiding from above; but it is difficult to convey the atmosphere of it to anybody who hasn't participated in an Eastern Orthodox Wedding.

Veronica was wearing a gorgeous long white gown and was very pleased with it all. A princess' wedding! Like a dream; and already in the past!

When they eventually went to Sitalkes' Temple (as it is called now), she didn't expect to be so moved by the experience. After all she had seen the photos and was prepared, she thought, of what was to come. And yet, she stood there overcome with emotion.

She knew the place, though she found it much altered. And it was not just because of the new wooden shelter covering it to protect it from the elements. And it was not so much because the landscape had noticeably changed either.

It was the feeling you get when you observe an empty stage, barren and abandoned, after a recent show where it has been bursting with activity. This is how Veronica felt having witnessed this place full of life, performing its full ceremonial role not so long ago.

She looked around her in dismay; it was a wonder that the Temple still existed and even though Time had not been kind to it, at least it had spared it. Veronica had to remind herself over and over again that although from her point of view, she had visited it less than twelve months ago, in actual fact it was a 25 centuries old edifice, what else did she expect?

Back then, the temple, built of massive granite blocks stood proud and imposing on the hilltop, not half buried in the ground, not derelict, not looted by treasure hunters, as she saw it today. And there had been treasures in it.

The statues guarding the entrance, now missing from their pedestals were not lions, as was now believed, but actually imaginary creatures, like sphinxes or rather griffins with lions' bodies and lions' paws, but winged and menacing with their sharp beaks. Veronica could picture them in her head. What had happened to them? Were they stolen in recent times or in antiquity?

The guide surrounded by a group of tourists was explaining something to them in Bulgarian and Peter was translating for her, so some things now became clear to her.

Apparently the temple itself had been discovered thanks to treasure seekers. They had dug into the mound and reached it from above, stealing the triangular fronton on top of the entrance door, but the temple had long since been emptied in ancient times and had been closed for unknown reasons. Another royal dynasty had come maybe and decided to send into oblivion a temple built by their predecessors. Such things happen.

The guide was pointing to the stone blocks of the façade, remarking that they were made of different stone, a lot smoother to the touch compared to the *crepis* and explaining that it was symbolic. They had been masterfully arranged without need of any binding element, which was the Thracian way (Veronica ran her fingers along the surface to feel the texture).

Next the guide and her group were examining the place where the double-winged stone door would have been set, the sight of the groove in the stone block made by the turning mechanism left everyone wondering at the technological progress these people had achieved so far back in the past.

Inside, in the round chamber, they admired the dome, the colour scheme, the half-columns, so many architectural elements which already existed at that time.

But Veronica had long since lost interest in the story. She did not hear anything new. She understood only too well how advanced these people were, far more than they were ever given credit for; she herself had seen that very door in operation with her own eyes and she had not found anything extraordinary in it at the time, because she had seen much more impressive sights than that!

And probably yet more of these edifices still existed somewhere in these lands, buried and forgotten, waiting for their hour to come.

Peter said: "But you are not listening! I thought you would be more interested!"

She replied: "In the end I didn't learn much from the guide; most of what she said, I knew anyway. That the Thracians were tall people, for example, judging by the height of the steps on the staircase, I've told you that already and also my theory about their diet; mainly dairy products; happily I love milk, so it suited me well! Also that the game from their hunting expeditions was making its way to the dining table and I must say I've never before appreciated so much the meat of wild duck or rabbit as I did in Old Thrace!"

"You have a point there about the diet, they reckon for example that the Japanese these days are also taller and bigger, as a result of more meat and dairy products in their diet, whereas in the past it mostly consisted of fish and rice. But you are unfair to the poor guide. She has not had the same advantage as you of being married to a Thracian king and to have first hand experience of the daily life of our Thracian ancestors!"

Veronica admitted that she was somewhat prejudiced, but in any case she had expected to find out more from this visit. Sitalkes Temple was still very much an enigma to her.

"And what's all this about treasure hunters? It seems that if it wasn't for them some of these sites would not have been unearthed at all!"

"Oh, true enough, but never the less, they are a real nuisance. More than that, it's all now getting out of hand. Treasure hunting has become a lucrative business and for some it appears to be their sole means of earning a living. The authorities mostly turn a blind eye, but don't miss any opportunity to greatly inconvenience the *bona fide* archaeologists, burdening them with all manner of rules and regulations. As a result, lots of valuable objects have been taken abroad to be sold to rich buyers and are now gathering dust in private collections."

"But surely that's against the law!"

"Of course it is! But who is there to enforce it? The customs officers complain that it's only too easy to smuggle out little knick-knacks in luggage; there are simply not enough resources to deal with this problem. Coins are the easiest to carry with you: ancient and contemporary coins are usually mixed together for a safe passage through security. And shortly afterwards they will be for sale on EBay! There you go! It's not such a harmless issue as it seems."

They did not manage to go to Perperikon that summer. Veronica was not sure that she wanted to go either. She had seen the pictures of the Rock city and she knew beyond doubt that it was indeed the Dionysus Temple that archaeologists were referring to. And she well remembered it in all its glory.

Its peak period, they said, was a bit later, when it became a palace and was significantly extended.

Alexander the Great and afterwards the father of Octavian Augustus were said to have consulted the Oracle there. It was still a thriving centre centuries later. Gold mines existed in the vicinity, the eyes of many different greedy leaders coveted it, so it was no surprise that it changed hands so many times.

Yet Veronica remembered how striking it had been when she saw it, towering up to the skies on that evening when she went there with Seuthes, all timid and awed to meet the Grand Sibyl.

That episode had made a lasting impression on her mind. She was reluctant to go there again if she was only to find the great Temple in ruins and a crowd of tourists taking pictures all over the place and carving their names in the rock.

That was a summer full of wonders. New archaeological discoveries were made almost every day on their very doorstep. Just outside the village of Shipka, 20-30 km to the north, new Thracian temples were excavated, yielding yet more golden treasures.

The most stunning find was a mask of solid gold featuring a bearded face that was said to be of Teres, Seuthes grandfather. A golden mask! Surely it could not be the same one! Or could it?

Each day brought some more news. The excitement of it! The impatience to find out more information! Veronica spent a lot of time on the Internet and read all the articles on the topic; most of them repeating the same thing, but she read on and on. She printed the photos. She spent time just looking at them.

Was it the same mask? Or wasn't it? Did it actually belong to Teres or to Seuthes himself? Whose was the face depicted there? She could not make up her mind.

What a fickle lady Memory is! How could one trust her? Veronica could not now clearly recall even Seuthes' features.

Later a statue was found revealing the impressive head of another bearded man; some said it was Zeus, others insisted on a Thracian king.

Could it really be Zeus? She saw it more like Moses, the way he looks on the famous statue by Michelangelo. Some reckoned it was the renowned Greek sculptor, Lysippus, who carved the head. Was that true? Wasn't it just wishful thinking?

Finally, it was agreed that the head of the statue must belong to Seuthes III, our friend of Seuthopolis fame. And he was surely a descendant of her Seuthes, very likely his grandson!

There were loads more artefacts apart from these. Veronica was also curious about the golden ring-seal picturing the so called "Olympic rower". It was discovered on the eve of the rowing competition in the Olympic Games, being held in Athens that year, and was dedicated to the Bulgarian rowers who were to take part.

Indeed it brought them luck. They did get a medal! But Veronica could not find a picture of the ring itself. Nobody took the notion of an Olympic rower on a Thracian ring seriously in any case, but at least somebody could have published a photo for the people to see for themselves!

In her own mind Veronica had already reached the conclusion that somewhere around there, in the triangle formed between Shipka, Maglizh and Kazanlak in the so called Valley of the Thracian Kings, was where Seuthes was buried. One of those tombs must surely be his. One day she would go and see the artefacts that had been found and she might, just might, recognise a ring, a sword, a helmet. She felt that she was on the right track.

Starosel and Sitalkes Temple were too far to the west, and

although there was a fair supposition that some of his family would have been buried in the vicinity, she did not believe that Seuthes was one of them.

Veronica was very distraught around the time of the funeral, but still, one is somehow aware of the surroundings no matter what. And she did not think it was there.

She had once been to the Temple of Sitalkes with Seuthes, true. But that would have been on one of their trips. Thinking more about it Veronica could even pinpoint it exactly, it was on their journey to Serdica to visit the young king of the Serdoi.

Besides, when she had gone back in time, she had found herself at an altar in the ancient town of Beroe; the palace where Seuthes had taken her to afterwards was not that far away.

The Roman villa, the foundations of which were discovered when building Peter's block, might have been built on the site of the ancient Thracian altar, and that would explain her appearance there – the trip would've been in time only, not in space.

So it could have been in the vicinity of any of the above places (Shipka, Kazanlak or Maglizh), which were at an easy distance from Beroe. And the horse's trappings were found not far away either, in her parents' garden, located in the village of Zmeyovo, the same area.

Veronica did not remember clearly where she had buried them; she had been so troubled that day. She knew she had gone for a ride, she had stopped at one point, she had prayed fervently to Candaon and then had dug a hole and placed them there.

The royal residence must have been in this area. But everything had changed since; 2500 years had passed! Only the mountains remained the same, but even their woody slopes could be misleading.

However, Veronica sensed she was on the right track. She

had solved the riddle to her own satisfaction in the end.

Reaching that conclusion, she became more light-hearted, more relaxed. She was back to the places where she felt she belonged. She actually thought that it was better that way, not to know the exact locations, nor to find Seuthes' burial chamber. Veronica preferred that he should be left to rest in peace, undisturbed by curious archaeologists and tourists or, even worse – treasure seekers; especially if his soul still lived on in some other dimension, called Afterlife.

It had been an eventful year this one. She had grown up, and, most importantly, she had regained her inner peace, lost at the time of her failures on the job front and the subsequent separation from James.

With the summer coming to a close, Veronica decided that she'd let too much time pass by and she should sit down to work. Peter was engrossed in another project, this time he was working on a hotel and did not have a lot of spare time.

"In the end this is the way I earn my living," said Peter apologetically. "You might've been a princess at one stage, but I can not offer you anything equivalent. A modest life style is all you will have with me, I'm afraid."

"Oh, Peter, I don't care for all that! One could be rich without the gold and the silver. I have had plenty of that already. It was Seuthes who mattered to me then. But he is gone now. And I have you instead. We could continue this journey of discovery together. It need not interfere with your work. First of all I'll sit down and write an account of what happened to me in ancient Thrace. I intended it to be a serious paper on the customs of the ancient Thracians, but now I reach the conclusion that it would be a mistake. I am not able to draw a general picture. And how am I going to explain my knowledge? I'll write a historical novel instead," she smiled. "In fiction everything is possible. And if there are truths in it, so much the better. In the end, Peter, from ancient times, people were handing over their experiences through the medium of tales and myths and songs. The ancient Thracians did not have their own alphabet, nor any written literature. This couldn't be helped. But at least I could try to make amends and write a story about them, from the point of view of an observer who lived 25 centuries later. While I'm writing, more bits of the puzzle might appear, so much the better, so much the better. New chapters would be added as time goes by."

GLOSSARY

Abdera, a town in Eastern Macedonia settled in the middle of the 7th century B.C. by colonists from *Clazomenae* and in 545 B.C. by the inhabitants of *Teos*.

Achilles, a Greek hero who took part in the Trojan War (cf *Iliad*) and lost his life in battle after being shot with an arrow in the heel by *Paris*.

Aesculapius, in Greek mythology the son of Apollo, god of medicine and healing.

Agamemnon, the king of Mycenae (or maybe Argos) who led the Greeks in the Trojan War (cf *Iliad*); he was the brother of *Menelaus* whose wife *Helen* was kidnapped by the Trojan Prince *Paris*.

Alcibiades (c. 450 BC – 404 BC) was an illustrious Athenian statesman, orator, and general. The last member of any renown of an aristocratic family that fell from prominence after the Peloponnesian War, he played a major role in the second half of that conflict as a strategic advisor, military commander, and politician.

Amadocus I (*Medoc*) was a Thracian king from 410 BC until the beginning of 4th century.

Amyntas, son of king Perdicass' brother, Philip.

Anaxagoras of Clazomenae (500 BC – 428 BC) was described as the last major Greek philosopher. He was prosecuted for impiety because of his political associations and his nonconformist ideas (he held for example that the sun was a blazing stone rather than a god). Died in the Ionian city of *Lampascus* near Troy.

Apollo, in Greek mythology the god of sun and light, the patron of art, medicine, archery, prophecy, defender of herds and flocks.

Apollonia Pontica, present day **Sozopol**, one of the oldest towns on the Bulgarian Black Sea coast. The first settlement on the site dates back to the Bronze Age. The town, at first called **Antheia**, situated in Thrace on the shore of Pontus Euxinus, was colonised by Milesian colonists. The main part of the town was situated on a small island just off the shore. The name was soon changed to Apollonia, on account of the temple dedicated to Apollo in the town. At various times, Apollonia was known as **Apollonia Pontica** (that is, Apollonia on the Black Sea) and **Apollonia Magna** (Great Apollonia).

Argos, an ancient city, situated just off the Argolic gulf at the northeast of Peloponnesse.

Artemis, **Diana**, twin sister of Apollo, the virginal goddess of hunting and patroness of the wild animals.

Atalanta, in the vicinity of present day Gevgelija in Macedonia, associated with the march of Sitalkes in 429 BC according to Thucydides.

Bendis, a Thracian Goddess whom the Greeks identified with **Artemis**.

Beroe (meaning "iron"), present day **Stara Zagora** (meaning "behind the mountain"), an ancient Thracian settlement and also known throughout its long history as **Augusta Trajana** (in honour of the Emperor Trajan) in Roman times, **Beroia/Vereia, Irinopolis** (in honour of Empress Irina) during the Byzantine period, **Boruy** (during the First Bulgarian Kingdom),

Eskizağra (Turkish for "behind the mountain") during the Turkish rule, **Zheleznik** (Slavic for "iron") in 19th century.

Bessoi, a Thracian tribe who lived in southern Thrace, a priestly caste, guardians of the Dionysian oracle.

Boreas, in Greek mythology the god of the North wind; his mother is *Eos*, the goddess of Dawn, his father is a Titan called *Astraeus* ("starry") and his brothers – *Zephyrus* (the god of the west wind), *Eurus* (the god of the east wind) and *Notus* (the god of the south wind); there was an ancient belief that *Boreas* and *Zephyrus* would dash down the mountains in spring and, taking the form of stallions, would mount the mares in the meadows; the foals allegedly born of such couplings were reputed to be the finest in the world.

Byzantium, present day Istanbul, was an ancient Greek city-state, which according to legend was founded by Greek colonists from *Megara* in 667 BC and named after their king *Byzas* or *Byzantas*. The name "Byzantium" is a Latinized version of the original Thracian-Greek name **Byzantion**.

Bizye, present day **Vize**, a Thracian city, a capital of the last dynasty of the Odrysians.

Calamis, a famous Athenian sculptor 5th, century BC.

Callias, one of the wealthiest men in Athens in the later part of the 5th century BC, descendant of an illustrious family.

Candaon, the name of the Thracian war god.

Cassandra ("she who entangles men"), in Greek mythology daughter of the Trojan king *Priam* and Queen *Hecuba*; for her beauty Apollo gave her the gift of prophecy, but for shunning him he put a curse on her, so no one ever believed her predictions.

Chalcidice (*Halkidikí*), one of the prefectures of Greece, it is located in the south-eastern portion of Central Macedonia; consists of a large peninsula in the north-western Aegean Sea, resembling a hand with three "fingers". In ancient times Chalcidice was part of Thrace. The first Greek settlers in this area arrived around 8th century BC.

Cholchis, in present day Georgia; ancient Greek legends told of a fabulously wealthy land where Jason and the Argonauts stole the Golden Fleece from King *Aeetes* with the help of his daughter *Medea*. It was a distant land that was reached by the Black Sea and down the River Phases. The actual site of this legendary kingdom has never been found but it is supposed to be somewhere in the region of Georgia.

Clearchus, the son of *Rhamphias*, was a Spartan general and a mercenary. Born about the middle of the 5th century BC, Clearchus was sent with a fleet to the Hellespont in 411 BC and became governor of Byzantium, of which town he was *proxenus* (consul). His severity, however, made him unpopular, and in his absence the gates were opened to the besieging Athenian army under *Alcibiades* (409 BC).

Cotys (*Cotytto*), a Thracian goddess worshipped with orgiastic rites, especially at night. Her worship was apparently publicly adopted in Corinth (c. 425 BC) and perhaps privately in Athens about the same time; it then included a baptismal ceremony. Later relief sculptures from Thrace showed her as a goddess of hunting, similar to Artemis.

Cyanean Rocks/Symplegates, the "Clashing Rocks" at the entrance of the Bosphorus.

Cyzicus, on the southern coast of the *Propontis*; connected with a famous naval battle in 410 BC; the Athenian navy led by *Alcibiades, Thracybulus* and *Theramenes* destroyed the Spartan fleet commanded by *Mindarus*.

Danaos, mythical king of Argos; from his name derives the name **Danae** applied to Homeric Greeks.

Dionysus, in Greek mythology the son of Zeus, he was god of wine and fertility; also known as **Bacchus** in the Roman pantheon.

Doberus, present day **Strumica,** a town in Macedonia, associated with the march of Sitalkes in 429 BC according to Thucydides.

Dorians, one of the main Greek tribes in antiquity; the others are Achaeans, Ionians and Aeolians.

Gortynia, present day **Gevgelija,** a town in Macedonia, also associated with the march of Sitalkes.

Hades in Greek mythology the brother of Zeus, he was god of the underworld and all things that earth has to offer; but also lord of the kingdom of death and the ultimate judge; also known as **Pluto** in the Roman pantheon.

Haemus, present day **Stara Planina,** the **Balkan range.**

Hagnon, Athenian military leader and democratic politician; in 429/428 BC an ambassador to the court of the Thracian king Sitalkes.

Hebrus, present day **Maritsa** River in Southern Bulgaria.

Hellespont, Hellespontis, in present times **The Dardanelles**, a narrow strait in northwestern Turkey connecting the Aegean Sea to the Sea of Marmara. Sestos is the city situated on the European side and Abydos – on the Asiatic side of this narrow channel. According to legend, Leander had to swim from Sestos to join his lover Hero at Abydos and it all ended tragically not unlike Romeo and Juliet. These two cities are also connected with the persian king Xerxes who, on his march in 480 BC, is said to have constructed a bridge across the Hellespont to move his cavalry across.

Hera, in Greek mythology the wife/sister of Zeus, queen of Mount Olympus, she was the protectress of marriage and women; also known as **Juno** in the Roman Pantheon.

Hercules, one of the Greatest heroes according to the Greek mythology, son of Zeus and Alkmene, renowned for his enormous strength; he went on to perform the 12 Labours and other heroic deeds; after his death he was deified.

Hermes, worshipped by Greeks and Thracians; but whereas the Greeks saw him as the messenger of the Gods, the patron of schools, trade, cattle-breeders, young men in general and also thieves and fraudsters; the Thracians believed him to be the protector of herds; the Thracian kings claimed that Hermes bestowed them with the royal sceptre, symbol of absolute power for he was associated with the Sun cult and the holy union of the Great Mother Goddess and her son i.e. the king to be; known as Mercury in the Roman Pantheon.

Hero *(Heros)*, the Thracian horseman god, depicted as a rider slaying a wild beast; seen also as the god of the underworld and usually found on funeral stelae; the term "heros" was appropriated by the Greeks with the meaning of demi-god, defender, protector and from there it passed into modern languages.

Herodotus of Halicarnassus, a Dorian Greek historian who lived in the 5th century BC **(484 BC – ca.425 BC)** and is regarded as the *"father of history"*. He is almost exclusively known for writing *The Histories*, a collection of stories (the Greek word histories meaning inquiries passed into Latin and took on its modern connotation of 'history') about the places and peoples he encountered during his travels around the Mediterranean.

Idomene, present day **Valandovo**, a town in Macedonia associated with the march of Sitalkes in 429 BC according to Thucydides.

Kazanlak, a town located in the Province of Stara Zagora, Bulgaria. The region around it has been inhabited for thousands of years, with traces of civilisation going as far back as the 2000 BC. A Thracian tomb dating from the 4th century BC was discovered here, near the ancient capital of Seuthopolis. Consisting of a vaulted brickwork "beehive" tomb, it contains, amongst others, painted murals representing a Thracian couple at a funeral feast. The tomb was declared a UNESCO World Heritage Site in 1979.

Lacedaemon, Sparta, is located in southern Greece. In antiquity it was a Dorian Greek militarist state, dominating the Peloponnese. During the classical age of Greece, they had the most powerful army in Greece. Technically, 'Sparta' was the name of their capital; *Lacedaemon*, was the wider city-state.

Lysippus, a prominent Greek sculptor from Sicyon, who also worked at Argos at the time of Philip and Alexander the Great.

Maglizh is a town in Central Bulgaria in the province of Stara Zagora; numerous Thracian tumuli have been uncovered in the vicinity.

Megarians, the inhabitants of an ancient city in Attica, Greece; they founded Byzantium, amongst other cities, in 667 BC; it is said of them:

"They build as if they are to live forever; they live as if they are to die tomorrow."

Nike, (pronounced "Nee-keh", meaning "Victory") in Greek mythology the goddess of victory; personification of triumph and success; sometimes depicted as a charioteer, sometimes holding a laurel branch or wreath, her wings suggesting the fleeting nature of victory; also known as Victoria in the Roman Pantheon.

Odrysians (*Odrisae, Odrusai*), the most powerful Thracian tribe, the only one to briefly unite all the others. Most Thracian kings mentioned in ancient texts were Odrysian kings. They were based in the central Thracian plain. Their names are often found in the ancient myths. Thus the Thracian singer *Thamyris* is said to have been an Odrysian (Paus. iv. 33. § 4); and Orpheus to have been their king.

Odysseus, the king of Ithaca, he participated in the Trojan War and came up with the idea of the wooden horse which caused the fall of Troy; his adventures on his way home after the war are the subject of Homer's Odyssey.

Orion, in Greek mythology a great hunter, who was killed by the gods and placed by them amongst the constellations after his death.

Orpheus, the son of a Thracian king, it was believed that his mother was one of the muses; he was considered to be the greatest musician and poet of antiquity; he would enchant animals with his music, compel trees and stones to dance. He took part in the expedition of the Argonauts, followed his wife Eurydice, who died after being bitten by a snake, all the way down to Hades and almost succeeded in claiming her back, captivating even Hades and his wife Persephone with his songs. He is also the founder of Orphism.

Orphism, a mystery cult dating from 6 BC; its followers were initiated during mysterious rituals, led ascetic lives, endeavouring to purify themselves; believed in the divinity of the soul and in afterlife: "I am the son of Earth and starry Heaven", you were supposed to say on reaching Hades and are not supposed to drink the waters of forgetfulness, but only those of memory, and then you will be reborn, Dionysus having redeemed you. There is speculation that Orphism may have affected the character of early Christianity.

Paeonians, the early history of which, like the boundaries of their territory, is very obscure. The Paeonians are regarded as descendants of the Phrygians of Asia Minor; large numbers of whom crossed over to Europe in early times. According to legend (Herodotus v. 16), they were Teucrian colonists from Troy, and Homer (Iliad, ii. 848) speaks of Paeonians from the Axius, fighting on the side of their Trojan kinsmen. At the time of Sitalkes, they were living to the west of the Strymon (present day Struma) river.

Pella, a town in Macedonia, close to Thessaloniki, the capital of the Macedonian kingdom in classical times.

Peloponnesus, the most southern peninsula of Greece as well as of Europe.

Perdiccas II (454 BC - 413 BC), a king of Macedonia.

Pericles (495 BC - 429 BC) the leading statesman of Athens for some forty years, during which period the city reached its highest point of power and glory. He was an able general, but was most distinguished as an orator.

Perperikon (also known as **Hyperperakion** or **Perperakion**) is located in the Eastern part of the Rhodope mountain range, about 15km away from the town of Kurdzhali. Perperikon perches some 470m above sea level, near the gold-bearing Perperishka River, irrigating the fertile lands that had attracted inhabitants for many centuries, which explains the numerous archaeological finds in the region. No doubt, the most imposing of these is Perperikon – a medieval fortress built on the site of an ancient Thracian sanctuary, related to the cult of the god of wine and feasts, Dionysius (known as Zagreus among the Thracians). As stated by some of the explorers of the site, this grandiose religious centre was built some 3,500 years ago and was used for ritual sacrifices of animals and people, as well as for religious ceremonies in honour of Zagreus. According to ancient authors the Temple of Dionysus in the Rhodope range was on a par with Apollo's at Delphi; there was also an oracle, not unlike the one at Delphi, who was famed for foretelling the fortunes of Alexander the Great and later predicting the great future that lay ahead for the newly born Octavian Augustus. Dion Cassius, a Roman historian, informs us of the capture of the famous Temple by the Romans in the time of Augustus; it was taken from the Bessoi and given to the Odrysians; which led to a war between the two, the Bessoi being led by the Oracle's High Priest.

Perseus, in Greek mythology a great hero, son of Zeus and Danaë, he was dispatched to bring the head of the Gorgon Medusa, a terrifying monster with snakes on her head instead of hair; he cut her head off while looking at her image in his shield; otherwise the sight of her would've turned him into stone. After his death the hero was placed in heaven amidst the constellations.

Philip, brother of king Perdiccas and father of Amyntas, he had challenged Perdiccas for the throne.

Pistiros, a major trading post in ancient Thrace, *an emporium.*

Plovdiv, a major city in Central Bulgaria it has previously been known as **Eumolpias, Pulpudeva** in Thracian times, **Philippopolis** (after Philip of Macedon), **Filibe** (during the Turkish rule).

Pontus Euxinus, the present day **Black Sea**.

Poseidon, in Greek mythology brother of Zeus, the god of the seas; known as **Neptune** in the Roman Pantheon.

Prodicus, a sophist and rhetorician from *Iulis* on the island of *Ceos*, he came to Athens where he became known as a speaker and a teacher.

Propontis, present day **Sea of Marmara**.

Rhaedestus (Rodosto, Bisanthe), present day **Tekirdag**, a Thracian settlement on the coast of Propontis, 78 km west of Byzantium; its bay is enclosed by the promontory of the mountain Tekirdag (known previously as Combos) which has given its present name to the town; Xenophon mentions it in "Anabasis" as being located in Seuthes' lands.

Rhesus, a legendary Thracian king who fought on the side of the Trojans in the Iliad. Later writers provide Rhesus with a more exotic parentage, claiming that his mother was one of the Muses, his father the river god Strymon, and that he was raised by fountain nymphs. Rhesus arrived late to Troy, because his country was attacked by Scythia, right after he received word that the Greeks had attacked the city. He was killed in his tent, and his famous steeds were stolen by Diomedes and Odysseus. The event is portrayed in book X of Homer's the Iliad and in the play Rhesus.

Salmydessus, ancient city on the Black Sea, erroneously located on the Hellespont in the myth involving King *Phineus* and the Argonauts. In gratitude for having retrieved him from the Harpies, *Phineus* advised Jason and his shipmates how to sail between the Clashing Rocks. This peril supposedly lay ahead of them, on their route between Salmydessus and the land of the Golden Fleece. But the real Salmydessus was beyond the location of the mythological Clashing Rocks.

Satok (*Sadocus*), the son of Sitalkes.

Scythians, people who lived to the north of the Black Sea, from the Don River, in present day southern Russia, to the Carpathian Mountains, in central Europe. They remained in power until displaced by the *Sarmatians* in the second and first centuries BC. They had no written language.

Selymbria (present day **Silivri**), on the Propontis' coast, situated strategically atop a hill on major trade routes; its natural harbor also contributed to its success.

Serdica, present day **Sofia,** known also as **Triaditsa** by the Byzantines and **Sredets** by the Slavs, exists from ancient times; the modern city of Sofia was named in the 14th century after the basilica St. Sofia (in Greek *sofia* means wisdom). The first recorded name Serdica came from the Thracian Serdoi tribe that settled here in the 7th century BC. Around 500 BC another tribe settled in the region, the Odrysians, who unified most of the Thracian tribes in their kingdom. For a short period during the 4th century BC, the city came under Philip of Macedon and his son Alexander the Great. Around AD 29, Sofia was conquered by the Romans and renamed **Ulpia Serdica**. It became a *municipium*, or a regional centre, during the reign of Emperor Trajan (98-117). The city expanded, as turrets, protective walls, public baths, administrative and cult buildings, a civic basilica and a large amphitheatre called *Bouleutherion*, were built. When Emperor Diocletian divided the province of *Dacia* into *Dacia Ripensis* (on the banks of the Danube) and *Dacia Mediterranea*, **Serdica** became the capital of *Dacia Mediterranea*. The city subsequently expanded for a century and a half, which prompted Constantine the Great to call it "my Rome". In the 3rd century AD, the Romans built strong walls around **Serdica**, their capital of Inner *Dacia* and an important stopping point on the Roman road from *Naisus* (present Nish, Yugoslavia) to Constantinople.

Serdoi, a Thracian tribe, settled in the region of Serdica.

Seuthes I (424 – 410 BC), an Odrysian king, son of Sparadocus, nephew of Sitalkes, whom he accompanied on his great expedition into Macedonia 429 BC. On this occasion he was won over by Perdicass, king of the Macedonians, who promised him his sister Stratonice in marriage and in consequence exerted all his influence with Sitalkes to induce him to withdraw his army from Macedonia; his effort succeeded and on his return to Thrace he was married to Stratonice according to the agreement (Thucydides. ii.101). In 424 BC he succeeded Sitalkes on the throne and during a long reign raised his kingdom to such a height of power and prosperity as it had never previously attained. The king's gold and silver coinage bear witness to the accumulation of wealth from the sale of agricultural and animal produce and the mining of metal ores. The Athenians sought the friendship of Seuthes I, so they declared him an Athenian citizen. He also maintained amicable relations with all the neighbouring peoples.

Seuthopolis was an ancient city founded by the Thracian king Seuthes III, and the capital of the Odrysian kingdom since 320 BC. It was a small city, built on the site of an earlier settlement, and its ruins are presently located at the bottom of the Koprinka Reservoir near Kazanlak, in central Bulgaria. In 2005 Tilev, a Bulgarian architect came up with a rather daring and futuristic project to uncover, preserve and partially reconstruct the city, making it accessible to the public. This is to be accomplished by building a circular dam resembling a well, of some 420 m in diameter circumscribing the pentagon shape of the city, sitting at the bottom of it. This ring is a physical as well as symbolic boundary between past and present, land and water, up and down. It will be the pier for boats, a walkway, a park, a whole tourist complex. The ancient city will be completely hidden during the boat journey from the shore, but on reaching the wall, the view from some 20 m height will be breathtaking. Panoramic lifts will provide access to the ground level. During the night the complex will be spectacularly illuminated. Whether this project will be realised, only time will tell. But if it is, ancient Seuthopolis will live once again.

Shipka, a village in Central Bulgaria near a celebrated mountain pass featuring a monument and church of the same name to commemorate the

Russian-Turkish war; in the vicinity of the village a tomb was discovered amongst other archaeological finds, containing golden artefacts, thought to be those of the Odrysian king Seuthes III; in the summer 2004 another burial place yielded more golden treasures and a solid golden mask which belonged, it is believed, to the Thracian king Teres.

Sitalkes (*Sitalces* **reigned 445 - 424 BC)** and was known as one of the great kings of the Thracian Odrysian state. He was the son of Teres, and on the sudden death of his father in 431 BC Sitalkes succeeded to the throne. He sided with the Athenians during the Peloponnesian War and attempts by the Spartans to change this failed. With an army of 150 000, Sitalkes and his allies invaded Macedonia in 429 BC in response to the Athenian request for help. He was killed during a conflict with the Triballi in 424 BC.

Sparadocus (*Sparadokos* **circa 445 - 431 BC),** son of Teres, brother of Sitalkes, father of Seuthes I. Reigned jointly with his brother until his death.

Spartacus, a gladiator, slave of Rome, who led an uprising against the Roman republic in 73BC-71BC; Thracian in origin, it is believed that he came from the present day town of Sandanski, Bulgaria.

Socrates (circa 470 – 399 BC) was a great Athenian philosopher who is widely credited for establishing the basis for all subsequent Western philosophy. As he spent his life acquiring wisdom and he left no literary legacy of his own, we rely on contemporary writers like Aristophanes and Xenophon for information about his life and work.

Stara Zagora, founded in ancient times (cf **Beroe**), now a major city and district centre in Southern Bulgaria.

Starosel, a village situated, near the town of Karlovo. In 2000, archaeologists discovered the largest Thracian temple-tomb in South-eastern Europe. According to scientists, it dates back to the end of the 5th century, beginning of the 4th century BC and was most probably intended for Sitalkes.

Stratonice, sister of Perdicass, the king of the Macedonians, given in marriage to Seuthes, the king of the Odrysians.

Strymon, present day Struma, a river in the West of Bulgaria.

Sveshtari (tomb of), dates back to the 3rd century BC and was included in the World Register of Historical Sites in 1985. It consists of three chambers - an entrance chamber and two antechambers. It is covered by a mound of earth. The decoration of the burial chamber is exceptionally interesting, a unique blend of art and architecture. The stone architrave, around the walls, is supported by ten caryatids. The wall opposite the door is painted in navy blue crayon.

Teres I, (reigned 475 - 445 BC) was the first king of the Odrysian state of Thrace. He was well-known for his military abilities, and spent much of his life on the battlefield. In 445 BC he died during one of his many military campaigns. He was later succeeded by his second son, Sitalkes.

Theseus, in Greek mythology a great hero, son of Aegeus, the king of Athens (or perhaps son of Poseidon himself) and Aethra, he went to Crete and killed the Minotaur, a monster with human body and bull's head, that lived in a Labyrinth (maze) to whom the Cretans sacrificed each year 7 Athenian maidens and 7 Athenian youths. Later he fought the Amazons and married their queen.

Thracian Chersonesus: 'Chersonesus' is a dry island, that is, a peninsula. The most famous being the Thracian Chersonesus, the peninsula separated from Asia Minor by the Dardanelles. Here is buried Helle, daughter of Athamas I, the girl after whom the Hellespont was named. The Thracian Chersonesus is the setting for the love story of Hero and Leander.

Thucydides (c.460- c.400 BC), Greek historian, born in Athens; took part in the Peloponnesian War, as commander of part of the fleet. He is accepted as the creator of objective historical science; he wrote "History of the Peloponnesian War".

Thynians, a Thracian tribe, occupying South-eastern Thrace in 5th century BC.

Tilataeans, a Thracian tribe, dwelling to the north of Mount *Scombrus*, present day Mount Vitosha.

Tissaphernes (c.445-395): Persian nobleman, satrap (provincial governor) of King Darius II in Lydia and Caria, belonging to one of the most important Persian families; at the time of the narrative, Commander in Chief of the Persian army in Asia Minor.

Triballi, one of the most numerous and warlike Thracian ethno-cultural communities. Their territory stretched from the far west to the northwest reaches of the *Oxios* River, present day Iskar. The Triballi, likened to "a swarm of locusts" when they were at war, were well known to the Athenians in the fifth century BC.

Vitosha, known in antiquity as *Scopius, Scombros, Scomios*, a mountain on the outskirts of the Bulgarian capital Sofia and referred to as the "lungs of the city" by locals; it is said the name **Vitosha** is of Thracian origin and means "with two peaks".

Zagreus, the supreme god according to Orphism, was said to be the son of Zeus and Persephone. At the instigation of Hera, Zagreus was torn to pieces by the Titans and when they proceeded to devour him, Zeus appeared on the scene. Driving the Titans back with thunderbolts he succeeded in saving the heart and gave it, still beating, to Semele to eat; subsequently the divine child Dionysus, the Greek god of wine, was born.

Zeus, in Greek mythology the father of both gods and humans, the king of Mount Olympus, the god of thunder, the protector of justice; also known as **Jupiter** in the Roman Pantheon.

Zmeyovo, a village in Central Bulgaria, in the province of Stara Zagora.

BIBLIOGRAPHY

Herodotus - "Histories"

Homer - "The Iliad"

Thucydides - "The Peloponnesian War"

Xenophon - "Anabasis"

Conon – "Narrations"

Pausanius - "Guide to Greece"

Diodorus Siculus – "Biblioteca Historica"

Cornelius Nepos – "Lives of Eminent Commanders", "Alcibiades".

Strabo – "Geography"

"Ancient Gold. The Wealth of the Thracians" (essays by **Alexander Fol, Margarita Tacheva, Ivan Venedicov, Ivan Marazov**)

"Starosel" by **Georgi Kitov**

"Perperikon" by **Nikolai Ovcharov**

"Monumental Tombs, Tomb Paintings and Burial Customs of Ancient Thrace" **Julia Valeva, Diana Gergova**

"Mednoto gumno na prabulgarite" (in Bulgarian) by **Ivan Venedikov**

www.ingramcontent.com/pod-product-compliance
Ingram Content Group UK Ltd.
Pitfield, Milton Keynes, MK11 3LW, UK
UKHW041437180426
11947UKWH00007B/490